PRAISE F(

"Stefan not only uses the 'shark' metaphor but has actually swam in shark waters to absorb the drama of life and death. He describes the attack strategems of a shark, but respects the intended victims enough to show how they can defend themselves. A stimulating read!!"
— *Philip Kotler, S. C. Johnson Distinguished Professor of International Marketing, Kellogg School of Management, Northwestern University.*

"You are swimming with sharks and you may not even know it. Stefan is your guide to not only surviving *Sharkonomics* but thriving in these adventurous economic waters."
— *Brian Solis, author of* The End of Business as Usual *and* Engage!

"Genuinely surprising and provocative – Stefan Engeseth has a streak of the evil genius."
— *David Magliano, Former Director of Marketing, London 2012 (Olympics).*

"Nature, red in tooth and claw, can be a great teacher. Stefan Engeseth has taken one of its lessons, that of the great sharks, and used it to present a view on strategy that pounces rather than plans and emphasizes movement over models. *Sharkonomics* is fast, ferocious fun."
— *Professor Alf Rehn, author of* Dangerous Ideas.

"Stefan Engeseth gets to the point again. Silent waters as well as markets are most dangerous in these days and we need to be proactive to survive."
— *Ritva Hanski-Pitkäkoski, President and CEO, Association of Finnish Advertisers.*

"This book has bite. It's snappy too. I urge everyone to get their teeth into it."

— *Stephen Brown, Professor of Marketing Research,*
University of Ulster.

"It is a sheer battleground out there; lots of 'strategies', 'tactics', 'attack plans'...*Sharkonomics* is not about survival of the fittest, but of the 'misfit' who has a streetwise cunning, coupled with imagination and creativity."

— *Nilgun Carlson, Senior Corporate Communications*
Manager, Oriflame Cosmetics.

"In this book Stefan dives in the deep blue to compare nature's natural way of hunting with today's business climate. Again he gives us a new way of looking at our own market and competitors; you need to dare to hunt to stay a market leader in your business."

— *Jenny Näslund, Marketing Manager,*
Comedy Central Sweden, MTV Networks.

"It's brilliant – to serve the result of millions of years of shark evolution for business. *Sharkonomics* develops one's instincts and loads of highly impulsive acts – but only for those who read the book."

— *Gisle Dueland, Marketing Manager,*
Turkish Airlines.

"Market leaders beware. *Sharkonomics* reveals the vulnerabilities and strategic insight needed to challenge leading brands."

— *Derrick Daye, Global Brand Strategist,*
Author and Branding Strategy Insider.

"Stefan Engeseth is brutally inspiring. *Sharkonomics* will definitely rock your boat. Or sink it!"

— *Jan Morten Drange, CEO, Norwegian Advertisers Association.*

"Catch a wave of the groundswell and surf the social web with *Sharkonomics*! Stefan Engeseth's book will take off and swim by itself."

> *– Martin Lindeskog,*
> *Blogger and Social Media Evangelist.*

"Stefan Engeseth offers a completely original point of view – rooted in centuries of natural history – to address an age-old problem. It is sure to challenge and illuminate how you think about competing in the marketplace."

> *– Kevin Lane Keller, Professor of Marketing,*
> *Tuck School of Business at Dartmouth.*

"Stefan Engeseth never fails to surprise. His logic of taking his inspiration this time from nature – with the simple yet poignant question: 'How have sharks survived for millions of years?' – has yielded a business book with teeth, and some pearly whites of wisdom."

> *– Jack Yan, CEO, Jack Yan & Associates and*
> *Director, the Medinge Group.*

"Stefan Engeseth leaves no one untouched and challenges once again with his new book *Sharkonomics*."

> *– Jan Fager, CEO, Swedish Marketing Federation.*

"One thing is certain. The companies that are not constantly moving and developing will sink to the bottom."

> *– Mariann Eriksson, Director of Marketing,*
> *World Wide Fund for Nature/WWF.*

"*Sharkonomics* gives you the tools to attack and to survive depending on where you are in the ocean of companies. Terrific and terrifying reading guaranteed."

> *– Jesper Ek, Head of External Affairs, Roche.*

"It's about time someone took competitive strategy thoughts to the phase of the 21st Century. Stefan Engeseth always has new and surprising angles on how companies should create enduring business success."

– Carl Wåreus, CEO,
DDB Sweden.

"*Sharkonomics* is a great companion for anyone in advertising dealing with market leaders and their competition."

Calle Sjoenell, Deputy Chief Creative Officer,
Bartle Bogle Hegarty.

"There's a fine line between genius and insanity. Walk the line with *Sharkonomics* if you dare."

– Micael Dahlén, Professor,
Department of Marketing and Strategy,
Stockholm School of Economics.

"*Sharkonomics* will inspire the retail business to move into new feeding grounds."

– Magnus Kroon, Director of Business Development,
Swedish Trade Federation.

"Market leaders: keep moving! *Sharkonomics* is a brand new view to the global marketplace."

– Eirik Hokstad, Chairman of the Board,
The Norwegian Market Society.

"He has done it again! Stefan Engeseth shows his knack for communicating the essentials of business success."

– Evert Gummesson, Professor of Marketing,
Stockholm University.

"Stefan Engeseth is always provocative and his new book cuts straight to the chase. Highly recommended to sharks (and their prey)."
— *Johnnie Moore,*
Author, Blogger and Consultant.

"Stefan Engeseth shares strategic tools in *Sharkonomics* for thought leaders in how to attack and how to defend your business in an ocean filled with sharks."
— *Luis-Daniel Alegria, Strategist,*
AKQA Berlin.

"Market leaders beware, domination is history."
— *Colvyn Harris, CEO, JWT India.*

"Stefan Engeseth is a marketing thinker and an entrepreneur par excellence."
— *Ami Hasan, Founder and Chairman,*
Hasan & Partners.

"Vital business insights from deadly sharks is what *Sharkonomics* provides."
— *Manoj Aravindakshan, Managing Director,*
On Target Media.

"Stefan Engeseth took a plunge with sharks so that we can open our eyes for blind spots to attack the market."
— *Akram Raffoul, Executive Director,*
Jacobsons Direct.

SHARKONOMICS
HOW TO ATTACK MARKET LEADERS

STEFAN ENGESETH

© 2012 Stefan Engeseth
Inside photographs by Stefan Engeseth

Published by Marshall Cavendish Business
An imprint of Marshall Cavendish International

PO Box 65829
London EC1P 1NY, United Kingdom
info@marshallcavendish.co.uk

and

1 New Industrial Road, Singapore 536196
genrefsales@sg.marshallcavendish.com
www.marshallcavendish.com/genref

Marshall Cavendish is a trademark of Times Publishing Limited.

Other Marshall Cavendish offices:
Marshall Cavendish Corporation. 99 White Plains Road, Tarrytown NY 10591-9001,
USA • Marshall Cavendish International (Thailand) Co Ltd. 253 Asoke, 12th Floor,
Sukhumvit 21 Road, Klongtoey Nua, Wattana, Bangkok 10110, Thailand • Marshall
Cavendish (Malaysia) Sdn Bhd, Times Subang, Lot 46, Subang Hi-Tech Industrial Park,
Batu Tiga, 40000 Shah Alam, Selangor Darul Ehsan, Malaysia.

The author and publisher have used their best efforts in preparing this book and disclaim
liability arising directly and indirectly from the use and application of this book. All
reasonable efforts have been made to obtain necessary copyright permissions. Any
omissions or errors are unintentional and will, if brought to the attention of the publisher,
be corrected in future printings.

A CIP record for this book is available from the British Library.

ISBN 978-981-4346-34-4

Cover Design: OpalWorks Ltd

Printed and bound in Great Britain by TJ International

This book is dedicated to the Great White Shark.

CONTENTS

Part two: 10 points for market leaders to defend themselves from shark attacks

FOREWORD

I first met Stefan Engeseth here in South Africa on a boat trip to study the behaviour of sharks. Stefan asked me why Nature had designed the Great White Shark so beautifully. My answer was simply that Nature's purpose was not only to design a beautiful creature; its main purpose was to design it for attacking its prey and defending itself.

When attacking seals, the Great White Shark can't fool around. Sharks hunt in an environment where their prey is almost as wily and fast as they are. Failure to catch and kill prey will mean the shark grows weaker and allows the competition to grow stronger. Compared to the world of business, Nature is arguably more competitive. In its battle for survival, sharks have discovered creative and strategic ways to rise to the top of their food chain. Their skills and strategies are the result of 420 millions years of evolution. After being around for such a long time, sharks know what it takes to be a successful and efficient predator.

Sharks and Nature are my passion. But I am also a keen follower of marketing and business. I share Stefan's view that there are strong connections between how sharks and corporations develop their strategies. *Sharkonomics* reveals how businesses can be improved and strengthened by learning from one of Nature's supreme predators. But in general, when you are with Nature, you learn so many lessons and realize how tough it is to survive in the wild. Businesses can't fail to learn something valuable from *Sharkonomics* and Nature.

Chris Fallows
South Africa

Chris Fallows is one of the world's leading experts in Great White Shark behaviour. His work is regularly featured on Discovery Channel, BBC, National Geographic and Animal Planet. He is the author of Great White and the Majesty of Sharks. For further information go to: www.apexpredators.com.

PREFACE

As a young kid back in 1975 I saw the movie *Jaws* and got scared just like everyone else. Back then fear made us believe that sharks were dangerous killing beasts. In a naive prank me and some friends built a fake dorsal fin that looked just like the fin on the back of a Great White Shark. We mounted it on my back and swam just off a crowded beach. It was a success. People were screaming and scrambling out of the water – but it didn't take long before they began chasing us!

Back then I thought nothing of it, but for that moment I had the pleasure of thinking and acting like a shark. During the last few years I have gone back to that feeling. Thinking like a shark has improved my business and helped me discover how to attack market leaders.

Steven Spielberg, the director of *Jaws,* is more famous. But Dr Leonard Compagno, who worked as the shark adviser to the movie *Jaws* and is not as famous, has published nearly 1,000 articles and several books on sharks. To track down this legendary shark expert is a bigger accomplishment than going on vacation with Steven Spielberg. To create a movie or a book in which sharks play the lead role is, however, no vacation – it is a journey that demands knowledge and input from experts such as Chris

Fallows and Michael Rutzen. Moreover, George Burgess, Director
of the Florida Program for Shark Research at the University of
Florida, inspired my journey with suggestions for books to read.

My knowledge cannot be compared to the knowledge of the
biologists and shark experts I have been "stalking", but certainly
my fascination and respect for sharks is far greater now than back
in the 1970s when I was that kid with a sense of humour.

How to attack the market leaders

For many years market leaders hired me to attack their businesses
in order to be ahead of potential competitors. On each occasion
I asked the CEOs if they had any restrictions for how I could
attack them and they always said "No!". They felt self-confident
and prepared for my attack. When I started executing the attack
in the workshop, the CEO usually started panicking after five
minutes, standing up and calling out "Stop!" and claiming they
did not hire me to attack from there but instead from another
position. Sharks will attack when the risk for getting injured is
small; if they injure themselves they will eventually become shark
food. Sharks eat sharks, especially if there is not enough food to
go around. Like a shark, I often attack from what I call the *blind
spot*: it is easy and it tastes good. The shark's way of doing market

research is quick and simple. Take a bite and if it tastes good the shark will continue its predatory behaviour. By that time it will often be too late for the market leaders to find protection. Most markets leaders are not willing to adapt to competition. Instead they will use their resources to get their lobbyists in Washington and Brussels to influence or help create laws that will turn *Jaws* into a vegetarian and stop the evil killing machine from rocking the boat named *Business as Usual*.

After *Jaws* came out millions of people suddenly preferred *not* to swim in the oceans[1] and instead swimming pool sales went up like never before. In their book *Freakonomics* Steven Levitt and Stephen Dubner explored such information connections. My ambition is not to change swimming habits but to connect the nature of sharks with business, which I call *Sharkonomics*.

It's not just about attack

In all my research about sharks, I noticed that about 90% of the information related to mankind's fear of sharks and their attacking abilities. However, even sharks recognize their own vulnerability and do not ignore the defence side. The same should be said for businesses, whether you are a market leader or a predator going after the former.

Therefore it made sense for me to develop a defence part in this book. It is also important to state that *Sharkonomics* is inspired by nature, but my intention is not to spread fear in any form except in boardrooms!

Stefan Engeseth
Author, consultant, speaker and
CEO at DetectiveMarketing.com ^{TM}

INTRODUCTION

Ever heard of a business author swimming with sharks?

In the name of research I challenged myself to jump into shark water – even if it was red and filled with terror. In the process of writing this book I took a scuba-diving certificate in order to go deeper with my research – sharks don't sit in boardrooms. To interview Mother Nature I had to "swim the talk". It should be noted that my publisher neither demanded nor recommended that I swim with sharks, especially not with the Great White. They were sincerely worried, but it might also have had something to do with the advance payment I got in book royalties. We have a lot to learn from sharks which are such fantastic creatures. I only hope they don't have a particular appetite for business authors. My intention was to learn from these highly evolved animals which play an important role in our ecosystem. Since sharks learn by stalking, I was going to learn from divers and shark experts.

Why *Sharkonomics*?

The Great White Shark became famous in 1975 with the release of the movie *Jaws*, but the movie's original story[2] goes back to 1916. Its scientific name is *Carcharodon carcharia,* but the Great White Shark was originally first named *Squalus carcharias* by the Swedish naturalist Carl Linnaeus (1707–78). Being similarly Swedish, I have come up with the term *Sharkonomics* for the business world.

The evolution of mankind is not as impressive as we think. Evolutionary scientists have pointed out how slow our evolution development has been. (I would also like to add that we have not been around for as long as sharks.) One of these evolutionary scientists, Steven Pinker, suggested that to speed up mankind's evolution we need to add technology into our bodies or pair up with another species. When I tested this idea in my lectures most people believed in the technology part but few felt comfortable with the idea of combining mankind with another species. This book is a combination of adding knowledge from another species and using technology to speed up mankind's evolution.

```
We have far more to learn from
nature, than nature has to learn
from us.
```

Nature is much smarter than the likes of Stanford, Harvard, MIT, McKinsey, Boston Consulting Group, Bain, IBM, Apple and all of the other *Fortune* 500 companies. In nature, sharks have to move to survive. But in business most market leaders do not, because they are stuck in history – and eventually become shark food. Sharks don't perform by producing endless Power Points; they bite into market share. *Sharkonomics* will reveal how the logos of market leaders will have more bites taken out of them than a seal after a shark picnic.

This book is inspired by Mother Nature's sharks which have been around for more than 420 million years and completed numerous strategic moves. It will prepare you to jump into the water and attack the market.

Economic competition is increasing rapidly and reduced resources will increase that further. Economist Joseph Schumpeter (1883–1950) came up with the term "creative destruction" to demonstrate why companies need to innovate constantly in order to survive. In my opinion Schumpeter was converting the saying "eat or be eaten" into economic terms. *Sharkonomics* is a further enhancement of this: "read this book and take a bite".

> "We will never really understand important economic events unless we confront the fact that their causes are largely mental in nature"
> — *George Akerlof and Robert Shiller,*
> *Animal Spirits.*

Taking a bite out of Apple

Apple shocked the mobile-phone market by introducing its iPhone. It was a classic wake-up call which saw Apple take big bites out of market leaders such as Nokia, Samsung and Sony Ericsson. The latter survived the attack, but it cost the company billions. When Apple moved into new territories with the iPad, it reported sales of millions. That is great, even by Steve Job's standard. But reporting the success of Apple is like pouring blood into an ocean, which attracts hungry competitors. It won't be long before the likes of Google will strike back with their own version of the *iPad killer*. Competitors act like sharks; they have a good sense for business and it will not take them long before they also enter the new market. Now the question is: How fast can Steve Jobs' successor swim before the sharks (competitors) catch up with Apple's advantage? A brand such as Apple can afford to take a bite in different business fields to see how it tastes: the iPod tasted good, the iPhone tasted even better, and the iPad made for a nice dessert. The music industry should have seen Apple circling around it years ahead of its attack. But where and what will the iShark attack next time? What will be Apple's next attack? With the iPad, Apple will continue its attack on the publishing business (books, newspapers, etc). But isn't it time someone attacked mighty Apple, for even sharks can be attacked? Apple is the kind of company that many people admire because they are outstanding in many ways, but the simple truth is that it is only good because the competition stinks. *Sharkonomics* will reveal where and how to attack companies such as Apple through some of the enormous blind spots they are unaware of and through mistakes in their defence strategies.

Do you dare not to read *Sharkonomics*?
Often you don't see a shark attack coming until it is too late. Don't let the competition strike and gain the edge.

Each attack will reduce the chances of survival for market leaders. The ambition of this book is not only to show how you can attack but also how you can defend yourself from upcoming attacks from competitors. You will learn how to use the fear of attack to inspire change by getting employees to swim faster to new territories.

Market leaders think their strength and size make a strong defence that can withstand attacks from competitors. But this is a false feeling of safety. Strength is only another form of weakness. Strength makes the blind spot bigger. When a shark attacks a big and strong prey, it simply takes a bite and lets its prey bleed until it becomes weak. Then the shark moves in for the final kill, which is often delivered with precision (on the core business).

In nature it is important to maintain a balance in the relationship between predator and prey. The prey which fails to adapt its defence system to the defence system of the predator will risk its market leader position. The predator which fails to adapt to new defences will suffer and lose a good meal of raw market share. It is called the "arms race between predator and prey". The attack and defence part of this book will inspire some major evolutionary changes in the nature of business.

The biomimicry lessons to learn

Nature is the biggest library of knowledge in existence. It has been around much longer than mankind and it will be there long after us unless we adapt. The biomimicry[3] field looks to nature for inspiration in order to solve known problems.

In issues such as gender equality sharks are way ahead of business. Amongst Great White Sharks the strongest and most aggressive gender is female. In some cases when male sharks don't show them the right respect, the females simply take a bite of their dorsal fins.

Business can learn many lessons from biomimicry,[4] even if I think many of the books are difficult to digest (but on the other hand sharks are famous for being able to digest almost everything).

> Corporations have to accept their mortality in order to survive; everyone in the market is in shark territory. Being in denial will be costly, no matter what business field you are in.

Biting into the corporate culture

Great White Sharks don't survive in captivity. The same goes for super talented entrepreneurs in big corporations. There are of course exceptions, but most of the time its only buzzwords used to attract talent in classifieds. I guess you wouldn't see a classified like this:

> `"Like the deadly jet fighter,`
> `the White Shark is graceful and`
> `powerful, sexy and frightening"`
> `    — Richard Ellis, Great White Shark.`

Just like Great White Sharks are born to be wild, super talented entrepreneurs do not survive in the corporate culture of today's market leaders. To manage raw talent, market leaders need to update their corporate DNA so that they can be *one* with the environment surrounding their business.

> `"Behaviour speaks much louder than`
> `words" — Peter Drucker.`

If the corporate DNA of market leaders is compatible with the nature of raw talent then this raw talent will help them to stay on the cutting edge of their sector. To achieve this, today's market leaders need to embrace a corporate culture that is graceful and powerful.

It is time to take a swim on the
wild side of business.

Market leaders are reforming

Market leaders are reforming and regrouping as a result of
the current economic crisis and market conditions. We are
already seeing some unusual combinations taking place – for
example, Microsoft is supplying software to Nokia mobiles.
It may not be long before we see Apple and Google working
together. None of the market leaders can survive on their own.
Predator companies should recognize that market leaders are
reforming and are working together to protect themselves and
their market share.

However, one thing is for sure: none of the above market leaders
have enough understanding of consumer power to avoid being
attacked by a predator whose moves are based on the currencies
that consumer power offers it.

Why *Sharkonomics* is not for everyone

Experts say that our fear of sharks is based on our fear of being
eaten alive. Since the purpose of this book is to eat market leaders,
alive in raw flesh and blood, it may trigger the same panic button.
I do respect and understand that this book may be provocative for
victims of shark attacks. Therefore, I strongly do not recommend

sensitive people suffering from shark-phobic tendencies to read this book or indeed visit *www.sharkonomics.com*.

Nature may seem brutal, but it is not personal, rather it is functional. Predators are just doing what nature has designed them to do – hunt and eat prey. This book aims to make it as natural for business to do the same – hunt and eat prey. Sharks may appear brutal when preying on their food, but their brutality is nothing compared to that of mankind. Mankind is practically feeding on and slowly killing Planet Earth, including killing sharks in a volume that can be classified as nothing less than a criminal act against Mother Nature.

A "clean cut" ain't personal.

Sharks attack with a "clean cut" and at first it doesn't hurt because it is so sharp and unexpected. In my opinion it is not personal, it is just business. I have improved my business a lot by learning from sharks. I have learned how to focus my business on what's nutritious for my profit and what's not. I have learned more about social structures and relations and how they function through studying sharks. However, a problem arises when I am swimming at my local swimming club. It appears I often bump into people in the pool. Of course, I have no intention of attacking my fellow swimmers but unconsciously these great sharks that I have been studying for a long time may have influenced me in some way. *Sharkonomics* will take a "clean cut" deep into the flesh of market leaders in order to take market share and move business forward into new directions. This book is not filled with fluffy buzzwords; its main purpose is to rock the boat (or sink it).

> Once again sharks will move out of
> the shadows, this time into the wild
> territories of the business world.

You don't like the sound of this? Read another book with beautiful diagrams and which doesn't contain deadly jaws. Please note: readers of *Sharkonomics* will embrace their feeding instinct and move around the market in search of prey to attack.

If you don't like the attack dimension in this book it could be a good idea to at least read the defence part so that you avoid becoming a victim of *Sharkonomics* readers who will do what the nature of this book has intended them to do.

> Nothing perfect is perfect.

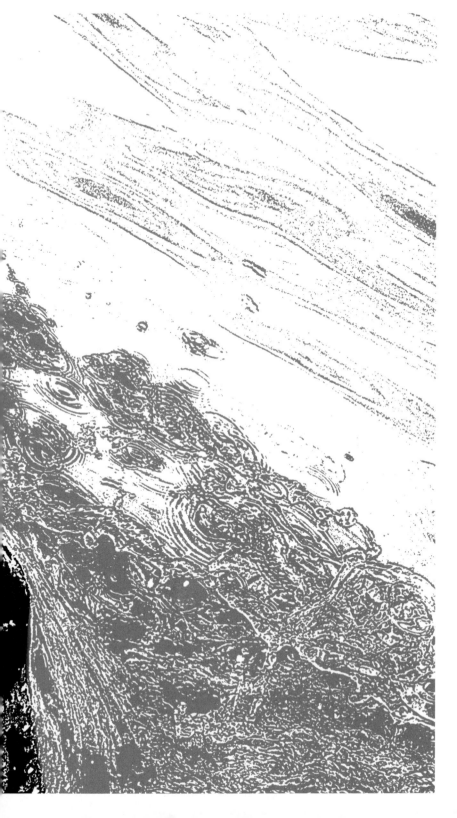

PART ONE

10 POINTS TO ATTACK MARKET LEADERS

1. Start planning long before your attack

2. Don't get stuck in history

3. Spread panic

4. Do market research the shark way

5. Find blind spots to bite

6. Strike unpredictably

7. Timing is key to successful attacks

8. Move or die

9. Kill with style

10. Write a Sharkonomics "attack list"

Start planning long before your attack

The bigger the corporation, the more narrow sighted it tends to become, with internal reality replacing the external one. Most of today's *Fortune* 500 companies can be compared to goldfish in an aquarium. Goldfish are famous for having a short memory whilst large corporations feel safe and invulnerable, which means that there is no need for either to "think outside the aquarium".

In studying several shark attacks we have seen that muscular alpha male is the first to jump into the water to save a victim. Is it heroic? Yes – but it may not be the smartest thing to do especially if you end up losing one or two limbs in the process. The reason they carry out such heroic acts of rescue is not to be heroic, it is simply that these alpha personalities are self-confident and don't think of themselves as being vulnerable. The same self-confidence in combination with a feeling of being invulnerable can be found in organizations with big strong leaders. These kind of CEOs don't consider themselves as the reason for their company's vulnerability. They organize everything around one key person; one who feels immortal and strong enough to take on any challenge. Yet all CEOs, with no exception, will become weak and old at some point. We end up seeing strong alpha leaders with their big egos jumping into the water desperately trying to save even the thinnest market share from attack. Market leaders think they live in a controlled, safe market position – but often they are nothing more than a large, chunky snack (with their guard down) for their competitors.

> ```
> Big corporations move slowly like
> turtles, and live on a false
> perception of being safe in their
> "big corporate shell". But the teeth
> of predators will bite into their
> shells like it's a biscuit.
> ```

Sharks have survived for more than 420 million years[5] and we will use this knowledge to stalk and eat those goldfish that try to hide in their aquarium-headquarters. In the shark world there is only one rule: eat or die!

Sharks are often called "killing machines", but I think most of all they are "learning machines". Over the years they have come to realize that if they stop learning and adapting, they will stop eating – and eventually die out. Business life is usually not as brutal as shark life, but still those who learn at high-speed will not only adapt but also, like the shark, be capable of feeding at the same time.

> ```
> Start planning your attack long
> before you execute it. If you don't
> know how you are going to attack,
> you may lose more than you gain.
> ```

Sharks have shaped their body to optimize their ability to hunt. Organizations have not even formed a body; instead they are stuck with core values and other nutritious buzzwords. Imagine this super-predator preying on these super-brands.

Predators are 100% focused on their mission. In business we often talk about the importance of creating an "elevator pitch" to sell our business idea in a quick and smart way. If we look at how elevators work they are not doing anything else other than what they have been built to do. They are designed purely to go up and down and they are focused on their delivery so that they don't waste energy. Because of their focus they don't need to be any stronger or powerful than they are. Sharks are enormously focused on what they must do and every step in their evolution has had the purpose of taking them forward to become a super-predator.

Often we like to compare ourselves with sharks. The golfer Greg Norman is referred to as "The Shark". Norman got his nickname for his aggressive way of playing golf, his size and his Australian origin. Today he has become a whole industry and provides a range of products and services from his website (www.shark.com). Moreover, numerous products, such as cars, are inspired by the perfection and beauty of the shape of the shark. Then there are the "Sharks of Wall Street" and law firms who have nicknames associated with the Great White Shark (fear has a market value). Others have developed a more sustainable connection to save the Great White Shark by adopting them – soon sharks may be swimming around branded with corporate logos and helping companies to take market share.

Is there really any market value in being compared to or connected with sharks? What can business learn from 420 million years of evolution?

Sharks use their superior senses to track down their prey. They are shaped like torpedoes, powerful and aggressive which makes it nearly impossible for their victims to escape if the shark has locked its senses onto it. For sharks, reading business magazines is not enough. The bigger a shark gets, the mightier the prey it will hunt. The size of the prey is in other words equal to the level of the shark's self-confidence and skills to strike undetected in a stealth-like mode (why waist energy hunting?).

> "There is no law of nature that the most powerful will inevitably remain at the top. Anyone can fall and most eventually do"
> — *Jim Collins, How the Mighty Fall.*

When sharks are stalking their prey they are merely planning their attack; but one wrong move by the prey and they will attack directly. Few authors have demonstrated more impressive research than Jim Collins has in his book *How the Mighty Fall*. Mr Collins reveals in this book how mighty corporations such as Bank of America, Motorola, Merck, Disney, IBM, HP and others nearly fell by making the wrong moves. In my opinion these corporations felt as unsinkable as the mighty *Titanic* which sadly ended up feeding the sharks. If there had been any readers of *Sharkonomics* around at that time, when the mighty were stumbling and making the wrong moves, most of them would never have survived. They simply would have ended up like the *Titanic*, becoming good-to-great-shark food.

Jim Collins' model below describes the five stages of decline: 1. Hubris born of success, 2. Undisciplined pursuit of more, 3. Denial of risk and peril, 4. Grasping for salvation and 5. Capitulation to irrelevance or death. In my opinion the model looks like a shark's dorsal fin.

The Five Stages of Decline

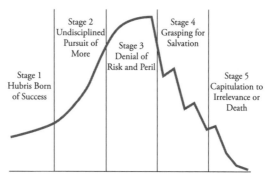

Source: *How the Mighty Fall.* Copyright © 2009 by Jim Collins.
Reprinted with permission from Jim Collins.

A good stage to execute an attack is in stage four. At that stage the mighty prey is weak and out of focus. This is the time for the predator to show its dorsal fin above the surface and spread fear and panic in the organization. When the prey is in denial about its mortality, it will not survive in the "grasping for salvation" stage, and will fall victim to a brutal predator attack.

I would argue that most corporations have made a lot of bad moves and nearly been killed in doing so. The only reason why the likes of BP, Toyota, Apple, Microsoft, HP, GM, IBM have survived is due to laziness on the part of their competition!

Remember to plan the attack by staking out your prey long before the attack is executed. This is important because a mighty prey is capable of mighty counter attacks. By stalking your prey and learning every stage of its decline, you will increase your chances of attacking even the mightiest company successfully. If the attack is done right, the chances of the mighty one making the right moves and recovering will decline. Unluckily for them, you will be tracking them and waiting for them to make their mistake.

```
Often victims will report they
did not even see the shark coming
towards them before the attack
occurred.
```

The mighty never learn

Up until now, they could afford not to learn – but now they risk ending up as shark food.

As soon as companies stopped listening to their customers/ clients, they were in trouble. I have been tracking this since 2004 and it's an endless story of bad moves on the part of these companies. But these mighty corporations never seem to learn – before it's too late. So when you plan your attack, look out for reports of dissatisfaction amongst customers both in B2B and B2C situations – this is your feeding time and your opportunity to grab market share. Jet Blue and South Pacific Airlines do this successfully by tracking other airlines' unsatisfied customers on Twitter and converting them into their own costumers. This is the stage before the prey starts to bleed (after this stage, you can expect a crowded shark picnic to take place). As well as B2B, attacks can work in B2C situations. Often described as "crowdsourcing", well-organized consumers can attack even the mightiest corporations by working in teams. Moreover, sophisticated corporations can combine consumer power into an attack that can be performed in different constellations (B2B2C or a B2C2B situation). With a common goal, anyone can team up for an good meal!

Don't get stuck in history

Many of today's market leaders are old corporations that have built their market share over a number of years. It is often said that it would cost too much to create many of the leading superbrands of today. In many ways that can be true. But since most of these old corporations are stuck in history, and are unfamiliar with new market opportunists, their defences are particularly weak against attacks from the future.

Most corporations are either stuck in history or not learning from it. Many of today's employee reward systems are built on short-term profits and returns. This pattern inspires leaders and CEOs to believe that corporations are born the same day they start working for them. By examining their past as well as their present you can learn about their patterns and build up knowledge about their weaknesses and strengths, and so predict how the market leader will try to defend itself from attack. In general market leaders have no, or a weak, defence to protect them from future attacks.

Start your attack far below the surface where market leaders will find it most difficult to defend themselves. Deep below the surface you will find trends and business opportunities from which you can create alternative solutions to that offered by market leaders today. When you are stalking your prey it is important to study the personality of the prey in the form of its behaviour, movement and, of course, weaknesses in its products and services. What have they been missing out on in upcoming trends in technology, green solutions, energy saving and consumer activity?

Sharks often wait for their victim to be separated from the pack – the odds are better when there is no one else around to provide warning of an attack. As soon as the gap between the prey and the pack starts growing, it becomes a good time to take a bite into their market share.

Clients and customers also form part of the pack. The separation from the pack is represented by their loyalty to the market leaders. And once these clients and customers become dissatisfied with the solutions offered to them, they will not offer any warning of an upcoming attack.

Market leaders that are stuck in history will eventually become shark food

Our nature defines how we act. If there is enough to feed on in a large home market, market leaders will often stick to what they have got rather than chase for more. This happens in home markets where there is a large number of people, strong economy or a market with various entry barriers.

In a global, transparent market there are no fences that can stop a hungry shark. Local market leaders or superbrands become obvious and nutritious targets to feed on. Shark experts are often fond of saying that where there are good feeding grounds, there are high hopes of finding sharks.

When sharks trespass into new territories, it is like walking into a buffet for them. No shark can resist a prey not anticipating an attack.

Positioning brands = easy targets

The old school of branding suggests that positioning is still working well for many brands. For sharks it is also working well because it means less territories to map out before attacking. Brands that are on top of the food chain feel safe and therefore are more willing to take bigger risks. Eventually they lose focus of their core business and leave their pack. Sharks often lie in deep, well-nourished grounds – whether this be an island or branding position – for good reason.

How to build good feeding grounds

If you attack too much in any given territory, it will make hunting harder. Your prey will be constantly on alert for potential attacks and the hunt itself can take up more energy than what you gain from the meal. You can stick around in a territory so long as you have mapped out your hunting ground for the future. But when the energy it takes to hunt exceeds the energy you gain from the hunt, it is time to move on. Moreover, moving away from and leaving territories to rejuvenate will result in nutritious feeding grounds for the next hunting season.

> "Life is a constant search for energy — the key to survival"
>
> — Dr Peter Klimley,
> The Secret Life of Sharks.

Sharks love eating so much that they sometimes vomit to enable them to continue their eating. It is not always the best thing to do because it can allow your prey to understand your pattern and get its protection organized. Never stay too long is a good way of building feeding grounds.

Why will China and India attack more effectively and globally

The short answer is: China and India have less modern business "fluff" in their history to protect. This means their management is more motivated to move to business fields that attract their senses for new opportunities. Don't believe me? Name one business field that Tata has not taken a bite out of yet?

Both China and India have cultures which are old and rich in history. They also have strong connections to nature and can move easily just like a predator to strike wherever the market is taking them.

Have you flown with Budweiser Airlines?

Probably not. Because they have been producing beer since 1876[6] and are firmly stuck on the ground. Unless their famous commercial phrase "What's Up?" actually is a hidden message saying that they are going into the airline business. I don't think that will happen for a long time – because they have too much history on the ground holding them back.

The last time I went to India, I flew with a modern airline company called Kingfisher. I did not know it then but later on I heard that they had started out as a beer company and expanded into airlines! I can imagine Kingfisher won't stop swimming until it eventually lands on top of Budweiser. And after that who knows where the Kingfisher will fly and strike?

How Google could sell tomorrow today

Today millions of people use online calendars to organize and synchronize the 24 hours of our days. But even when we have digital support we don't seem to have enough hours to manage our lives. Wouldn't it be great if Google Calendar could offer increased life quality, more hours and make millions at the same time?

Imagine today in your calendar you are typing in your family holiday to Las Vegas on a certain date. How much would it be worth to you to not spend days searching for all the relevant travel information that is needed for this trip? For Google AdWords it is worth millions. With a connection to the calendar your future could be searchable. There is no question that advertisers would be willing to pay for AdWords in your calendar – the question is how much will they pay for it? There will be no need for you to go to Yahoo to make a search because all the answers would be available in your personal Google Calender. Some people would argue that this would be getting too personal. But if Google and others were able to offer added-value in your life (for example, managing your time more effectively), you are more likely to accept this kind of intrusion into your privacy.

Google could create a scale from 1 to 10 for people to choose from in terms of how much information they want to receive. 1 could be no information; 2 could include travel information; 3 could be suggestions for discovering new things located in where you live; 4 could be different choices for creating meetings with people; 5-7 could be more personal and be on a coaching level; 8-10 could be information to change your life at a level that can be compared to the movie *The Game* (where reality and fiction combines to challenge your personality and development).

Advertisers could then match their offers with the behaviours of millions of people who have chosen to move and travel. For example, constructors could offer repairs of homes and cars when their costumers are travelling.

Costumers today know their value and with the above scale they can have the power to choose how many hours they would like to get out of their travel and everyday life. By opening up your information, you get greater quality of life in return.

Making money out of privacy is not the idea. Instead the idea is not to let advertisers know who you are – only to connect behaviour with offers. Let consumers have the power to control the level of information and consume if they so wish to.

Some good movers

Not all market leaders are stuck in history. Because we don't see their history, we often don't see their track record of the moves that they have made. Instead, we have come to believe they have been in their current position for a long time.

Here are some good movers from the recent past:
- Lamborghini use to make tractors – today it is one of the market leaders in sports cars.
- Nokia use to make rubber boots – today it is one of the market leaders in mobile phones.
- Yamaha use to make pianos – today it is one of the market leaders in motorcycles.
- Virgin Records use to make records – today it is one of the market leaders in virtually every territory Richard Branson chooses to move into.
- Several outsource manufacturers used by market leaders – today they have moved from the shadow and out on to the surface by offering their own brands directly to the market.
- Despite their rich history, if such companies stop moving and seeking new territories, they themselves can become targets for predators to attack.

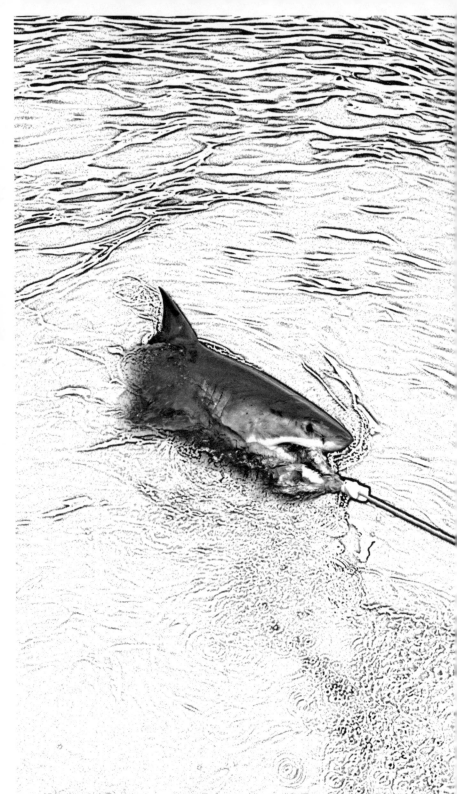

03 Spread panic

When its dorsal fin slices through the water and the predator starts to move around the market leader, decisions will be taken in moments of panic. Most market leaders will not have enough space to enable them to move out of the way of the striking shark. Prey do not move well in a panic situation and will pay the ultimate price for it. A skilled hunter will terrorize its prey with fear; even a rumoured attack will make them lose focus on their business goals.

We all react differently to fear. Some of us freeze, others panic, some simply run away, while others fight back. For sharks fear is the ultimate weapon and they sense it in others as a sign of weakness. Experienced divers have told me stories of how sharks have tested them – if the diver reacts with fear it could well trigger an attack. For sharks, one way of testing divers is to sneak up on them from behind and when the diver turns around they will be standing eye-to-eye with a shark often three or four metres tall! The shark will not be shouting: "SURPRISE!" Instead it will be checking if you are controlling your heartbeat or if fear is controlling you and telling the shark that this is an easy meal. Imagine conducting this test on top management and market leaders. If they behave in a frightened way, it can trigger the shark's instincts to attack. Remember: spreading fear takes less of the shark's energy than the attack itself.

The chances of getting attacked by a shark are close to zero

Yet we still fear sharks with passion and fascination. *Why?* Our survival instincts prevent us from becoming served as shark food, so naturally we don't want to expose ourselves to the possibility of becoming a victim for a violent shark attack. But what if *you* could become that well-armed killing machine that is the Great White Shark, with a weight of two tonnes and a length of over six metres? Then you could feed on victims suffering from laziness, which is what most market leaders are. In fact after only one bite of a *Fortune* 500 company, fear of the next attack will make this market leader lose its focus and, eventually, become even more vulnerable. To survive, the other 499 companies should read *Sharkonomics* to find out how to avoid becoming shark food. Some may even hire real shark guards from Down Under to work in their headquarters' reception.

Without fear most believers would not believe

Today's business life is stuck in history. Up until now it has been better to protect the old ways of doing things than to embrace creativity, innovation and change over time. But the old ways of doing things have finally become too old. The reason why most corporations do not adapt to new times is simply because they do not need to. There is no meaning in investing money in development if the company is successful. But the market has now become transparent and consumer-smarter. The Internet gives both businesses and consumers the possibility to organize themselves collectively and demand better products and services. Finally there is no other choice for corporations but to change things. Out of fear of losing share, market leaders are now motivated to adapt. When the unmistakable black triangle fin starts to circle outside headquarters, fear will make any market leader believe in change. Fear can be used to motivate big organizations to embrace creativity and innovation. Even the dorsal fin of small sharks will create fear in big organizations. Hopefully it will inspire employees to think outside the box – effectively putting the shark in the corporate aquarium.

Sir Richard Branson's attack-itude

Whatever business field Mr Branson goes into he spreads fear. *Why?* Because his strike record is a bloody story. Sharks are born killers: they don't go to school and they don't need their parents to show them how to eat. They pop out and start to feed on what's around them; they are born with a natural instinct to attack. The shark's attitude – best described as "attack-itude" – is one where it moves around its prey with high self-esteem and confidence. I am sure British Airways realizes that Sir Richard Branson's attack-itude is a natural born gift.

Mr Branson has a witty and captivating personality that makes his prey underestimate his striking capabilities. When I had the honour of finally meet Mr Branson, I could immediately sense his attack-itude. His "Virgin shark" has become big and strong. The bigger this "Virgin shark" has become, the more self-confidence it has built up to attack bigger prey. Today Virgin is so big that it is capable of attacking any business in any sector.

When present territories are no longer challenging to attack, Virgin moves on to markets that do not yet exist – like space travel. Being a serial entrepreneur gives Mr Branson the advantage of moving into new territories long before the competition can understand what is happening – and when they sense the attack is coming, it's usually too late.

"The demands for innovation has
never been greater"
— *Sir Richard Branson.*

How fear can create change

The Virgin shark has spread fear into every business field it has
moved into and to others that are waiting for its shark fin to show
up in their headquarters. Those who handle fear in a positive
way will find that it can be a strong motivation for change
management (ask British Airways).

Sharks are not built on fluff, they are as hard as steel for both
attacking and self-protection. Sometimes sharks attack boats or
they jump three meters above the water surface and land on boats,
which can cause boats to sink. This happens rarely but even if the
chances are small, and it is not the way sharks behave normally, it
creates fear that can be used to improve change in management.
The predator will sense fear and set change free.

Fear is a fast way of killing
conservatism and works both
internally and externally.

Do market research the shark way

04

Most of today's products, services, corporations and brands belong better in a museum than in the market. Market leaders are far behind in terms of what a transparent market demands. By working with traditional market research they are losing speed and are becoming easy targets for a predator attack.

Why waist energy and time on prey that do not taste good or lack nutrients? Sharks certainly don't do that. But in the corporate world we seem to waste enormous amounts of resources and time on market research that only result in poor profitability and slow development.

Market research can result in profit in the future, but if sharks operated as ineffectively as most market leaders do when using market research, they would become extinct. Keeping up with changing conditions in nature is crucial for a species' survival. To be able to compete with other species, sharks need to adapt faster than others if they want to stay on top of the food chain. To do so, they have developed a solution called "test bite". Similar to wine tasting, it's a way of investigating the prey by letting our sensory system examine and evaluate the prey. It can certainly be faster than reading a report six months after the window of opportunity has gone by. Neither sharks nor sommeliers become experts by only reading. Instead they taste everything and whatever doesn't taste good they will spit it out.

Finding prey with good odds

Whether you are operating in the B2B, national or international market, the market space is potentially wide-reaching and large. In fact, it's too big, and it makes it easy for prey to escape. Sharks don't like hunting under such short odds. So they move and find places and situations where the dice is loaded in their favour.[7] For example, they hunt in shallow water where it's easy to corner their prey (unless it's a bird). Moreover, bad visibility turns any water into a buffet for the shark. Sharks also like to attack lonely prey, which has separated from its pack – the prey that has no one to warn or protect it. So, you should search for good odds when biting.

Why the hidden side of evil is good

Sharks will just open their jaws and slice into their prey; if it taste right they will carry on with the attack on their prey. Many experts claim what often saves human beings from such shark attacks is that we just don't taste that good and are not the most nutritious meal to be found – so sharks move on. Market leaders, however, almost always taste good, are high in nutrition and full of market share. If they don't taste so good, you should just move on without wasting any energy or time. The more aggressive a shark is, the faster it will learn to develop new and improved attack strategies.

> "Kill the adoption barrier and you are already on the market"
> — Dr Alexander Osterwalder, advisor and author on business model innovation.

Test and stress competition

In the corporate world many large companies are not aware where their arms and legs actually are, and are not well synchronized, which makes them an easy target. One quick way of finding out how they will react is to take a test bite. If nothing happens it is a free meal and if you are lucky they will lose both arms and legs before they fully realize they are under attack. The most common reason why corporations have poor defence systems is due to poor organization. Another common reason is that management has not kept up with changing conditions in the "nature" of their businesses. They just don't get what's worth protecting. They are stuck in old-school thinking and believe that the only value a company has is how it directly can be valued in money terms. In a transparent market there are many other critical values, such as internal and external loyalty, tribes[8] and consumer power. Corporations need to develop more ways to increase value creation in other currencies besides money.

> "Attention is our primary currency"
> — Linda Stone, legend of
> the digital revolution.

When you are testing and stressing out the competition with a test bite, you will learn how the market leaders will react, which in turn will reveal the strengths and weaknesses of the market being under attack.

Test bites v killing bites

For many years Apple's fans demanded a mobile phone. To be able to make calls with their beloved iPod was a natural development for such fans. At that time Apple neither had the resources nor knowledge to develop a mobile phone from scratch. Corporations such as Nokia, Motorola and Sony Ericsson were market leaders then and ruled the mobile market with self-confidence.

When Apple took its first test bite of the mobile market, it did not want to risk too much so it only put iTunes into a Motorola mobile phone. When Steve Jobs pitched this solution to Apple's consumers at one of his legendary keynotes, the audience went quiet. *Why?* Because this mobile phone did not anywhere near live up to the fans' expectations – many thought it was not a real Apple product.

It was not a total failure. It was only a test bite to enable Apple to evaluate the effort of moving into the mobile phone market. It tasted good but Apple had to go back and digest what it had just learned and blend it in with the reactions of their fans.

Apple could have stopped there with only a test bite (on many occasions sharks do that, especially if the victim moves away from striking distance – but market leaders bleed more than they move). Instead Apple came back and this time it was a killing bite – in the form of the iPhone. When sharks attack elephant seals they often bite off a large part of their fin (hindquarters), which is an effective way of stopping the prey from swimming off. In business the equivalent could be stopping the market leader's cash cow products and services. Apple took a clean bite deep into the product-fin, which slowed down the mobility of the mobile phone market leaders. Its killing bite was the perfect answer to the dreams of Apple's fans (and the rest is history). Where are Nokia, Motorola and Sony Ericsson today? Well, they are not for sure market leaders anymore. Instead they have been following Apple and its iPhone, feeding on its leftovers or copying its leads and moves.

Few brands are bigger than their corporation, but Apple is one of these few. It means that the demand for the brand is much greater than what the corporation is delivering today in products and services. Fans are willing to follow it into new territories and its brand is capable of swallowing much more market share than it is doing now. Apple could strike out and turn up in virtually any sector. Instead of the iPhone it could have come up with iCar or iFly. Other corporations don't know how big their brand can become because they don't move into new territories. Instead they have to wait for a predator to come along and take a test bite out of them.

Blue water to red

Half a decade ago, *Blue Ocean Strategy* was released and became an international bestseller. W Chan Kim and Renée Mauborgne's book offered a "short-cut strategy" idea to making competition irrelevant. Instead of going head-to-head with competition and fighting a battle over market share in the bloody red ocean, companies should find new blue oceans where there is less competition.

It was an easy idea to sell, but much harder to make work in reality. Firstly, there is almost no blue ocean left to explore (or prey to feed on). Secondly, many corporations that find themselves in "blue oceans" are in fact out of their comfort zone, in the sense that they lack the skills and knowledge to take advantage of opportunities and end up making the wrong decisions.

Back in the days when there was time to innovate and develop a position slowly, the blue ocean idea could have worked. But today, in a transparent market, that kind of strategy will turn most corporations into shark food.

Kim and Mauborgne based their book on a study of 150 strategic moves in 30 industries over a period of 100 years. *Sharkonomics* is based on sharks which have been around for more than 420 million years and made billions of strategic moves. Blue water has become red and it's time to change strategy. Sharks don't care what colour the water is when they attack and feed.

In red water, moving is not an option

After Apple performed its brutal shark attack on the mobile market, the water became red and filled with nutritious opportunities. This triggered other sharks to join Apple in this new feeding ground for a meal. It maybe like jumping into a shark tank – but it doesn't matter because everyone knows that when the boat is rocking it can lead to profit. At that time Google entered the market with its mobile software Android and it may soon follow that with its own gPhone-version. High-end technical providers such as Huawei and ZTE from China, Samsung from South Korea and HTC from Taiwan are also entering the red waters. Others, such as Nokia and Microsoft, will try to team up to become bigger and stronger again. As I mentioned earlier, in times of danger former market leaders are more motivated to form alliances.

There are always tangible opportunities for those who seek them. Like when the iPhone had security problems, which would have been a good time to attack Apple. In such a situation, it is often better to move in for a killing bite rather than a test bite. HTC or Samsung had the opportunity to take the lead from (read: kill) Apple.

Find blind spots to bite

Prey often sense their own vulnerability
and protect themselves from attack
from most angles. But when the prey
and predator move in a trial-and-
error relationship, new angles will be
revealed. The shark is looking for blind
spots to take a bite without risking a
counter attack.

Predators are constantly searching for prey. They are always improving their hunting techniques through trial and error. Stalking may not have the purpose of attacking, but it can bring knowledge for future hunting success.

Sharks can spot a drop of blood in a large swimming pool. Swimming without focusing on the money is a waste of energy and resources. This book aims to equip the reader with the mindset of a shark and teach the reader how to hunt down market leaders and eventually become their worse nightmare. Follow the money and your feeding instinct will lead you to the core businesses of your prey.

Swim around to find a blind spot, because most prey are not focused on their core business. They then often become vulnerable and compensate for this by trying to become something they are not. By starting to swim around it from far off and gradually closing in, without risking detection, you close in on your prey, find the right blind spot as well as learn about your prey's feeding habits, strengths and weaknesses. This is the "G-strategy" for attack (see Figure 1).

G-strategy

Moreover, your stealth-like mode will prevent a counter attack from your prey. What do market leaders do today when they enter a new market or expand to different business fields? They send out press releases, which has the same effect as pouring blood into the water. It only attracts other sharks and eventually your attempts to gain market share will cost you more energy and money than necessary.

There is no way for your prey to protect itself from what it cannot see and hear. Success is a mixture of timing and stealth.

How to attack Apple – bite-by-bite

Once Apple was a challenger, today it is a mighty market leader. In the beginning of the book I promised to reveal where and how to attack Apple in some of the enormous blind spots it has, and to mark out Apple's mistakes in its defence strategy.

In many ways Apple has grown into a Killer Whale, which is an apex predator capable of killing even a Great White Shark. Killer Whales are social and live in family systems. Apple's family system consists of its different products – computers, iPods, iPhones, iPads and services such as iTunes and App-store. Apple's blind spot is growing because of its successful development. The company is moving into the stage where success increases the *denial of risk,* as pointed out by Jim Collins in his book *How the Mighty Fall.*

By feeling invulnerable Apple is in fact increasing its blind spot, which makes it easier for predators to ambush it. One way to do this is to lure it in by leaving its favourite meal swimming as wounded prey ("an offer it can't refuse" also works well in the kingdom of nature). Since the Killer Whale is dangerous, a good idea would be to take a first bite out of the Killer Whale's back fin (for Apple this could be the distribution of iPhone). Without its back fin it can't move and will eventually drown and sink. After the attack it is important to move out of striking distance from the family members and wait until they move on. The first member of the family has been served as a meal; the others can come later.

The market is full of "iPhone killers" in the form of brands such as HTC and Samsung, but potentially the most dangerous predator attack on Apple could be delivered by Google (with Android, Google has learned many lessons in how to attack the mobile market). Google also has a family of solutions and its corporate DNA is closer to consumer power (in this case, its open source culture). Apple has a lot of fans but currently its relationship with them is based on a monologue instead of a dialogue. For Google this is an opportunity to gain power over thousands of communities who love Apple but who have not yet received a reply from Apple confirming their passion for the brand. Google can start the attack by following the currents in its fan tribe and attacking from an angle it has not thought possible before. This could mean Google using Apple's own costumers against it by doing things superior to Apple in every part of its solution and being *one* with the costumer.

A part of that attack could be to create a situation where Apple is forced by consumer power and opinion to let go off millions of credit card numbers it has obtained from its costumers (privacy and freewill could be two questions to build the opinion on). This will remove Apple from being just a click away from its costumers.

What do you think are the five best killer applications Google should develop to attack iPhone and Apple's share in the mobile phone market?

06 Strike unpredictably

A shark that is predictable will eventually become a victim itself. Endless training combined with superior senses makes the shark an effective and deadly attacker. In business, striking unpredictably can also be the difference between "eat or be eaten".

Often their prey will think that sharks will not attack in places that seem less than logical, when in fact sharks often attack precisely when and where their prey least expect it. Not expecting a shark attack at certain locations makes the prey less cautious and therefore more inclined to take risks. The *Sharkonomics* way is to find unexpected and illogical locations to deliver an attack and do the unexpected. By planning and locating places and business fields that market leaders don't think of or even know of their existence yet, you can deliver unexpected attacks. Surprise is often best served raw.

How to ambush an unsuspecting market leader

Market leaders who hire me to attack their business always feel self-confident and prepared for my attack. But after five minutes they panic. *Why?* They think I should attack them in places where they have good defence, but sharks attack where the chances of an easy meal is best served – where the defence is at its lowest. Most management teams are stuck in their comfort zone. This creates unlimited space for predators to enter new territories and ambush market leaders when and where they least expect an attack.

Over the years I discovered many ways to spot with ease the weaknesses of market leaders. Often people disagreed with me, but after a bite or two, they painfully came to realize and understand their vulnerability. Here are some ways to bite into fleshy market leaders. If it is an IT/Internet company, you can immediately assume that IT/Internet is getting old. Whereas once it was an innovative and a vital business field, today it is no longer that. Instead the IT/Internet sector these days is full of old solutions and bureaucratic organizations. In other words, the organization has grown from innovation stage to a stage where the growth of new fields has been held back by old fields and interests. One example is mobile applications – this would have grown much faster if there where no "old" computer interests to protect. This is also the reason why places such as Africa is faster to adopt mobile Internet (they don't have any old behaviour to replace – everything is new for them).

Technicians are technically strong in the solutions they build for the online world, but they often have enormous weaknesses in understanding the offline world (so I attack from the perspective of offline). If it's an offline company, I reverse it and attack from the perspective of online, etc.

A good way to attack both an online and offline company is to move between online and offline – market leaders have enormous weakness here and most of them will not even see the attack before it is too late.

Facebook and such market leaders will in time come to understand this, but when I interviewed some senior managers from Facebook's London office, they did not see that yet. Facebook will soon have over one billion members and I can see a Facebook credit card working online and offline, and literally changing the world of economics in the near future.

The following are some lessons for attacking in an unpredictable, shark-like way.

Shark lessons from the secret service

After delivering many lectures around the world, I wanted to try out a new format of lecturing. So I invented and started to organize "Unplugged Speeches", which consists of lectures free of PowerPoint, laser pointers and distance. The goal is to focus on the meeting and proximity to people as well as the content. When the fifth Unplugged Speeches took place we had as the speaker Thom Thavenius. Thom is a former employee of both the Swedish security and intelligence services and has unique knowledge of the field of intelligence analysis and strategy development. The audience consisted of heavy-weights from the likes of Google, Spotify, Universal Music, Swedbank, Nordea, TV4 and others. The goal of the lecture was to discover lessons from the secret service and how the business world could use them. Thom delivered knowledge about how to spot patterns and how to use that knowledge internally (in marketing, leadership and change management). Thom talked about how leadership in an organization can navigate by understanding and using the best available information there is to get.

When I interviewed Thom prior to his lecture and then listened to his lecture, I discovered that the business world could not only learn to connect the dots in the present, but also to connect the dots in the future.

Corporate market leaders do not set much value on discovering what is happening in their environment; for them, it's just good to know. However, when you are working in life and death situations, as with the Secret Service, you are probably more motivated to take notice of how the world is changing.

Shark lessons from hackers

All systems are built to fail. *Why?* Because they are constructed on logical knowledge from our history. Today these systems are easily attacked by, for example, hackers who see through the construction of our systems.

Hackers are in the business of breaking things down and putting them together again. Hackers may not have the education and background that the business world demands, but time and again they have proven to be much smarter than the best educated IT minds. Corporations are built like IT structures with logical patterns which make it possible to hack and bite into the code of its core business. Hackers and sharks have a lot in common: they move in unpredictable patterns and simulate numerous attacks to discover their victim's weakness before moving in for the actual attack.

The security surrounding today's IT structures is not a challenge for world-class hackers to break through. In an interview Paul "Pablos" Holman, who used to be a traditional hacker, showed me how poorly the security was working. His computer skills and personality led to him being nicknamed "the Madonna of hackers".

Pablos has a positive mindset: he is now trying to use his talent to "hack into nature", and change the way nature reacts. He is studying how hurricanes such as Katrina and diseases such as

Malaria and Polo could be controlled by hacking into nature's processes to control or stop them. He is also working on trying to solve challenges such as energy, food and other big issues of our world.

Pablos is a hacker who uses his skills in a positive way. But all hackers have a gift to see patterns and their weaknesses, which gives them an edge when striking unpredictably in business. Both hackers and sharks are searching for those weaknesses to attack.

Find a common goal

Sharks are good team players but there is always a risk that they will feed on their fellow team-mates if they are left with no other option. Developing common goals is a way of getting internal resources to focus their energy. It is good to combine this with the G-strategy of attack – for many predators a fast meal is a safe meal, for the longer time it takes to eat a big prey, the greater competition will increase (blood attracts more competition).

Hunting big prey like sea lions and elephants can be dangerous because such big prey can counter strike. One way of getting around this is to take a test bite. The test bite will usually weaken the prey prior to you moving in for the precise killer bite. In business, social media is a great team tool for predators to detect opportunities to team up for feeding opportunities.

Eye witnesses have reported seeing seven Great White Sharks working in unison to move a dead whale away from the beach to feed on it in deeper waters. There are several market leaders that are just like the whale stranded on a beach, waiting for a team of predators to move it safely into deeper waters. Who said sharks weren't social creatures?

Shark lessons from social media

The classic recommended steps to get started with social media are: listen, learn and participate (this works fine for sharks, too). However, the hype surrounding social media is so enormous that it risks losing its connection with reality. Brian Solis' book *Engage* points out this risk: "The social media universe is in danger of spinning off course and into a black hole of obscurity." Brian's passion and search for answers has lifted social media to the academic level.

Guy Kawasaki is one of the best practitioners of social media. In my opinion he is an expert at "destroying resistance" – his personality is really hard not to like. As he says in his book *Enchantment*: "Push technology brings your story to people. Pull technology brings people to your story."

Being a good listener is a combination of buzz and social media; it's the same as developing a sensory system to find and attack your prey. It is just like Brain Sollis pointed out in a lecture: "The listening tells you everything."

Shark lessons from buzz

Talking about something we believe in gives us social values that make us willing to buzz about it. This is also one strong reason for why "open innovation" is so successful – people believe in the products, services and brands they are a part of. As Gary Vaynerchuk, in his book *Crush It!*, said: "Getting people to talk is the whole point."

The success of buzz today is mainly due to the online world. Sharks live offline but their behaviour and visual uniqueness makes them worth buzzing about online. With this in mind I interviewed Emanuel Rosen, the author of *The Anatomy of Buzz* and a leading figure in the field of Word-of-Mouth Marketing. Emanuel is a down-to-earth person and does not assign the online world much importance. For instance, when I got a bit too excited about the digital world during our interview, he stopped me and said: "Stefan, look around you, what do you see? Do you see anything digital?" As I looked around the hotel lobby I came to understand his point.

He continued, saying that we talk about the online world but we still live in the offline word, which has enormous impact on our day-to-day life. In the future the online world will become bigger (new technology will appear everywhere). Nevertheless today's physical world around us is much bigger and important for how we build buzz. Emanuel elegantly pointed out the following: *"The big question is how to build in technology into old structures."* He added that the physical world is strong but the digital connection is extremely important for creating buzz.

We also discussed why people talk about things. According to Emanuel it gives us status in the tribes we live in. When I asked why some people buzz more than others, Emanuel pointed out that some are "hubs" (I call them "radios") who send their message to many people around them. There are two kinds of hubs: expert and social hubs. The expert hubs want higher status by being known for being an expert. Social hubs see it as a way to connect with others. It is also a way to make us unique and stand out from the crowd. When everyone knows about something there is no value in buzzing about it. Saying what everyone already knows will not make you stand out. In other words, to get hubs buzzing you have to confirm and strengthen their identity. Their currency is information and if they have high credibility people will listen to them. (Although if they speak in favour of a corporation they will lose their credibility and people will turn away from them.)

A word Emanuel uses often is "relevant". Every part of the story (including the corporation and the hubs) must be relevant for everyone or else the story will be irrelevant to talk about. My interpretation is to find a radio channel that both the sender and receiver are willing to listen to. There is a limit to what we believe, but if we believe in enough of it, it will give us social values worth talking and buzzing about.

Being creative is one of the strongest ways to build buzz. If you involve consumers in the creation of a solution, they will become enormously engaged in it and therefore also more willing to spread the word. But Emanuel also highlighted the risk of listening too much to the most engaged consumers, who often want extreme performance. I asked Emanuel if that meant these engaged consumers wanted sport cars? "Yes, more or less you could say that and the normal family person who is buying your cars often need a family car."

07

Timing is key to successful attacks

Shark victims often report that they did not know what had hit them. If you were to ask the shark, it would say that it was the perfect time for it to strike. By painting "the market picture" well, you will recognize what will happen in the market long before market leaders know what has hit them.

There is water in every part of the world but there is no meaning being in places where there is no prey to eat. Often sharks follow ships for long distances, and by doing so, makes it easier for the sharks to clock a meal by being in the right place at the right time. (Translation: market leaders are the big ships, full of potential market share to attack.)

Every year the sharks show up at the same time, just as their favourite meal enters the water outside South Africa's False Bay, and are seen swimming around Seal Island (named after its prey, as you could probably guess).

Since sharks are ambush-hunters, the timing of their attack depends on certain conditions (such as visibility) and which gives them an edge in striking undetected. Not many corporations have a success rate as high as that of sharks. This is simply because sharks know more about their prey than corporations do, who most of the time view prey as something fluffy in a CRM system (numbers are not flesh and blood!). Have you ever heard of a CRM sales pitch saying: "Take a bite at the right time at the right place"?

Timing is easy when lunch is served on the Ring of Death

It would be a "bite" harsh to state that the problem of management today rests on top management and CEOs. Instead perhaps what we should be asking is why "business as usual" has survived for so long? It's like on Seal Island in South Africa. During World War II, huts were built on the island made of materials brought in from far away. This is the island where a large population of seals come to each year. And when that happens, the largest number of Great White Sharks to be seen anywhere turn up. When the seals enter the water to feed, their main predator welcomes them by jumping five metres above the water surface. Called the Ring of Death, the sharks proceed to circle their prey. Much of management fail to realize they are living in those huts and that they are being stalked whenever they enter the water.

The seals may not live in the huts but management still do in the form of old strategies. But today the huts are a just a few ruins like badly positioned market leaders. When Apple attacked Nokia it was the iPhone that jumped high above the market surface.

Using social media as a sonar system

In a transparent market both predator and prey gain from good visibility. Good visibility is not by itself an advantage (it has to be combined with something else, such as ambushing in stealth-like mode). Social media works like a sonar system where it is easy to investigate your prey long before an attack is executed.

If a predator knows the agenda of its prey, it will be easy for it to predict the prey's next move. Social media such as Facebook and Linkedin together function even better than the shark's senses. Through social media the prey not only reveals its behaviour but also what it is doing currently and what it will be doing next.

What would sharks write about on Facebook?

Sharks bump into each other in the same way that we poke each other on Facebook. Sharks are more practical and so would talk a lot about different prey and feeding grounds (as we talk about restaurants and food); they would talk about mating (as we talk about dating); they would organize themselves into groups based on status levels (as we build tribes around status, brands, titles, business class, etc); they would talk about their enemies (as we do about our enemies and sometimes politicians); and they would talk about different territories of feeding (as we talk about travelling and absorbing different impressions). In other words, you could add sharks to your friends list and have quite a lot to talk about to them.

Most people would rather have a shark as a friend than the opposite. Because we live in such a connected world, the consequences of such "poking" can be significant. Social media is like wine tasting – the more you know, the better it will taste.

Headhunting in a new dimension

Not so long ago in mankind's history headhunting was about brutally taking a person's head off. Often heads were removed from the enemy and shown off to your tribe and the rest off the world.

In our more civilized times, we no longer take heads off when headhunting. Instead we bring them into the tribe and then often hide them from the rest off the world.

One main reason why traditions have shifted in headhunting is simply because companies today find greater value in using the heads of talented individuals rather than showing them off. But I would argue that we still use heads just like in the old days, in the way companies bring them into the tribe and show them off to the modern world. These heads are highly valued by the business world because they influence stock value and tribe value. Those heads with high market value are used to show off to the media and the world how important the market leader is. The visibility of these heads makes it easy to find and hunt them down. This way of modern headhunting is widely used in the business world as well as in the search for country and political leaders.

The big thinkers are often not the ones displayed officially on the surface – they are usually kept far below the surface providing IQ and knowledge. Many of the really talented employees are never shown to the rest of the world. It is inside the heads of these big thinkers that the development and future of the corporation can be found, which is one reason why corporations try to hide such heads in departments such as research and development.

Sharks attack the big prey in the most effective way possible, such as biting at the propeller dorsal. If you are a predator in business trying to win market share from the leaders, find the right heads and win them over. And by using social media, you will find the right timing to strike without revealing your purpose.

Move or die

If a shark stops swimming it will die. Most market leaders believe they are moving but they are not. In the current waters it is dangerous just to float around when the jaws of death are moving far below the surface.

Even before sharks are born they have to compete to survive. Some shark species can have as many as 25 babies. To survive, these sharks have to cannibalize their babies and as a consequence only one of the 25 survive.[9] Modern science has revealed that predators often practice cannibalism for practical reasons. Their own species is easy to find and have the nutrition they require.

Cannibalism is also common in the business world. In a market that has reached saturation point, one company will be bought up by another competing one and will be called a merger. Oracle swallowing up MYSQL is a form of survival in the competitive marketplace.

> "The nutrition you need the most can best be found in the same spices"
> — Professor Volker Rudolf,
> Department of Ecology and Evolutionary
> Biology, Rice University.

Motivation is pure power

Sharks are at one with their environment, which gives them the power and movement to strike. Predator sharks propel themselves by moving their tail back and forth. An airplane's tail uses forward movement to push air around its wings to create capacity for aerodynamic lift. Sharks do the same with their fins to push water around them in order not to sink. They are practically flying underwater.

If that is not enough motivation to keep them moving nature has designed the shark's breathing system in such a way that it will stop functioning if the shark doesn't move. It would simply drown and sink at the same time.

Have you ever heard a motivational business speaker say something like "move to stay alive"? I doubt it – but that is the natural law of doing business.

Moving is learning

By always being in a trial-and-error mode and modifying your stalking strategies to attack different types of prey, you will enhance your adaptability. Never miss out on a dinner because your prey has better escape tactics than you. Companies which continuously move will learn more and create change in its management – and therefore avoid getting bitten.

> "How much will it hurt, if we do not move?"
> — Sara Öhrvall, Senior Vice President, Research & Development, Bonnier.

In oceans everything is connected and constantly in movement. To be a part of "nature's movements" it is crucial to coordinate yourself with the current, sun, temperature and so on. For sharks, the sun and shadows play an important role in helping them remain undetected. By moving undetected, it's easier to strike and more difficult for your prey to predict your attack.

Speed generates strike power

Sharks are so muscular in their build that their human victims often describe an attack as if being hit by concrete. It is true that they have hard bodies but as it is with cars, it is the speed that generates power. The power of the collision takes the air out of most shark victims or makes them go unconscious. Such strike power can be increased with disloyal or unsatisfied clients and consumers when attacking the market leader. Moving upstream takes more energy, so move in the same direction as the current of consumer power in order to gain more speed. Such consumer power can be unsatisfied consumer tribes found online in social media. Currents can be trends or major changes such as materials, behaviour, Corporate Social Responsibility (CSR) or anything else that builds up a demand for change.

MySpace fans created SharkSpace

MySpace came to realize that even its most loyal fans can turn against it. Market leaders that are arrogant, speak in monologue and fail to deliver what is demanded can result in disloyalty. They risk even their strongest customers defecting. And since fans are close to each other, it was easy for them to create damage fast for MySpace.

Often market leaders upset their fans when they are not moving in a direction the fans feel is important (which is easy in today's hierarchical organizations). Unfortunately I discovered this myself when, as a costumer, I sent suggestions to YouTube. I got no response but later on I discovered that they did the opposite of what I had suggested. The reason for doing the opposite could of course have been due to other factors rather than my suggestion. But a fan doesn't usually see it that way; instead the fan will take that passion away and move on to another market leader that listens and supports him/her.

From fans to enemy-hooligans

The media have reported that fans of soccer teams are behaving strangely. Violence is nothing new in soccer, but this time soccer fans are directing their anger against their own teams! *Why?* Because they don't think their team is performing in the way they should, so they have transformed from fans to enemy-hooligans. I think we will see the same phenomena repeated for many brands; their fans will turn against them if they believe the brand is not delivering what it should. If brands don't deliver or score goals of innovation, fans will simply revolt online and offline in shops and perhaps even in the headquarters. *Why?* Brand leadership means never standing still; always running for the next innovation or development. If fans of one brand experience other brands as being better, they will transform into enemy-hooligans and go against their own brand. Brands that have seen this happen include MySpace, Ericsson and Levi's. Apple could become one of them because Apple does not in my opinion understand how fast it must run its innovation when it has so many passionate fans. A predator company could certainly use this to its advantage.

How Skype and Spotify spotted a free meal

A market leader that is not moving is provoking an attack by being a meal too hard to resist. It takes less energy to hunt it down and has plenty of fat market share, which is irresistible for any predator company.

As author Chris Anderson reveals in his book *Free*, free is a good way to create spreadability and word of mouth. Skype and Spotify created products that resulted in two high-in-demand services being used for free, which also attacked the market shares of the mighty leaders in the telecom and music industries. This strategy literally slaughtered the market leaders which eventually gave in and tried to run away from the attack. But it was too late – both Skype and Spotify had established their territories.

Working 9 to 5 worked well in 1920 but will not in 2020

Moving 24/7 works well for sharks and will work well for corporations that want to move with the times and not miss opportunities. Speed and constantly being in an innovative stage of changing and adapting is what enabled companies such as Google, Cisco and Groupon to grow into global predators.

In young corporations, and in fields such as IT, it is easy to move faster because history is not holding them back. Also, new feeding grounds attract employees who have a mindset focused on being adaptable. Raw talent focused on adaptability will move on to other corporations if they don't think their current corporation is moving fast enough to satisfy their personal development.

> "If you have a long time view, good things will follow"
>
> —Kaj Arnö, Chief Evangelist, MYSQL.

MYSQL was an open source database corporation which at one time had over 10 million followers. At that time the market leader Oracle simply was not able to move in the same evolutionary speed. There is not much defence against such quick movers as open source solutions, so Oracle implemented the classical

American defence move and bought MYSQL. It cost it billions of dollars, because first Oracle tried to buy MYSQL directly, but when that didn't succeed Oracle bought Sun,[10] which recently had bought MYSQL. Catching up with fast movers is costly and it can also lead to cannibalization of the sector. The future will tell if Oracle can manage to get 10 million people to follow it – they are not for sale.

09 Kill with style

Do sharks have a sense of humour? Well,
for sure they are having fun doing
what they do well, hunting and eating.
Predators often play with their victims
in order to show off their raw power and
superiority over their victims. A smiling
shark is a well-fed shark.

Enter new markets high above the surface

Ambushing from below with a high-speed attack is a surprise technique. In the arms race between the predator and its prey the shark's adaptability is the key for successful hunting. Seals taste good and are nutritious but they have also developed strong escape strategies. To increase its success rate sharks use nature's resources to their advantage. In such cases sharks hunt when visibility is poor and start the attack far below the surface, striking its prey on the surface like a torpedo – often their speed is so fast that the shark jumps above the surface with its prey in it jaws. Surprise with style is a good way for predator companies to enter a market.

How Apple could jump into the sky with Boeing

During a long distance flight I got bored and turned on the movie-screen mounted on the seat in front of me. I could not get the movie to start from the beginning, so I asked the stewardess for help. Her response was: "This is the last trip we are using this airplane – when we reach our destination today we will turn this airplane into scrap." I have to say that was funny. But I could not stop thinking of other newer options for aircraft entertainment. Old airplanes feel more out of date especially when the inside looks old and unsafe – it needs to be as updated as other parts of our digital life. If I see it, others will too.

Why is Boeing not working with Apple to install iPads in every seat? It could save Boeing millions and at the same time make its aircraft entertainment edgy. That will make long-distance flights feel shorter. Consumers will spend so many hours with their iPads that they will get addicted to it. For Apple it would mean lifting sales even higher than perhaps the legendary Steve Jobs managed to do. The benefits for Boeing would be saving money as well as creating new income by making Apple its partner. Also it would be easy for Boeing to update its aircrafts by changing from iPad 2 to 3 or 10 in the future.

It could also create a webpage with the airline brand and apps for Boeing. Other commercial partners could join in: EA for games, Hertz for cars, Amazon and Barnes & Noble for ebooks and of course various travel-related companies.

After I blogged about this idea (I called it iFly), Boeing Twittered about it. Flying experts around the world responded quickly. The current of this idea seemed to grow. The same airline which I took my long-distance flight with, Finnair, is one of those airlines that is planning to take a test bite on iFly. If Apple doesn't ride the iFly current, then maybe Samsung Tab will and attack a multi-billion shopping market. The potential lies in those millions of customers flying boring hours with nothing else to do than to get entertainment and shop. This predator attack can and will change the game for one of the largest business fields in the world – the travel industry. Why? Because iFly will influence consumers to choose not only what they might consume when they land, it will also influence where they might travel next time. Moreover, these same passengers will influence their friends by using social media and buzzing to them to check out their travel advice from 10,000 feet above. Combine iFly with Google Earth, Facebook and Twitter and it could become a game changer for the travel industry.

Attacking from the clouds

Today a lot of business sectors – such as finance, CRM, bookkeeping, data storage – are protected because of the large

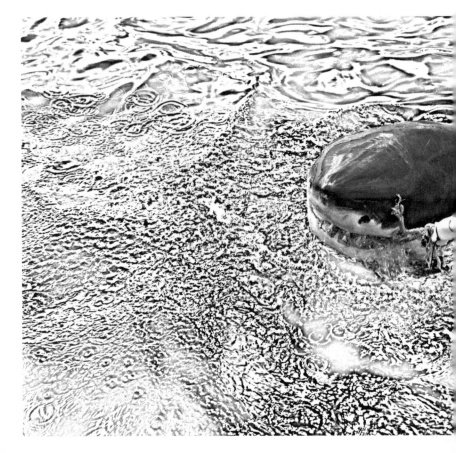

investments required to develop them. They have grown safely into market leaders because their competitors have been unable to make the necessary investments to compete with them. But now as these IT investments move into the clouds, there will no longer be any obstacles to protect market leaders from competition – for clients and consumers it means freedom of choice.

As a result, predator software companies will move up the food chain, devouring market share in sectors such as finance. Services previously protected by barriers of entry will no longer be a problem for such predators.

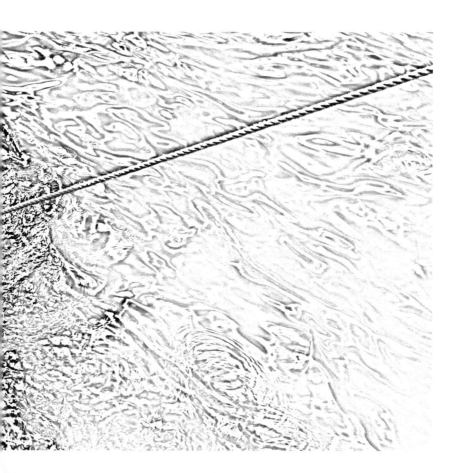

Write a *Sharkonomics* "attack list"

A shark that doesn't find its prey will starve and eventually die. Sharks that focus their energy on nutritious prey will grow larger. There is no point being mean if it doesn't pay off! Eventually all market leaders make a wrong move; if a predator company is following them, it could be their last move.

How to find nutritious prey to attack?

1. Go online.
2. Search the *Fortune* 500 and read it like a gourmet menu.
3. Pick your meal on the menu.
4. Start working on your moves by starting to use the *Sharkonomics* attack list from step one.
5. After you have eaten a market leader, cross out its name on your *Sharkonomics* attack list.
6. Always bear in mind, if you swallow too much big prey, you yourself could end up on the list (but being on the *Fortune* 500 list would be a nice achievement).

Who are your top 10 prey to attack?
1.
2.
3.
4.
5.
6.
7.
8.
9.
10.

Then move on to attack the rest of the 490 that are left on the *Fortune* 500 list.

Why are these prey the best ones to attack? What would you learn, achieve, risk?
1.
2.
3.
4.
5.
6.
7.
8.
9.
10.

Evaluate if this prey is nutritious enough to attack. If not, choose another on the list, or just take some time to stalk and date the prey (it's good to know what you are eating in the future).

What are the market leader's blind spots?

1.
2.
3.
4.
5.
6.
7.
8.
9.
10.

What are the "killer bites" that you can deliver when you are in the right position?

1.
2.
3.
4.
5.
6.
7.
8.
9.
10.

Always do more than this list and never ever stand still. Hungry for more? Take a bite at *www.Sharkonomics.com*.

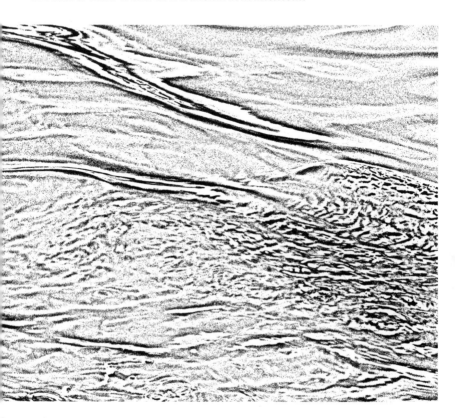

PART TWO

10 POINTS FOR MARKET LEADERS TO DEFEND THEMSELVES FROM SHARK ATTACKS

Introduction: Defence

1. Develop your defence strategies years before you get attacked

2. Never stand still

3. Let others spread the buzz

4. Don't panic when under shark attack

5. Find out where your blind spots are

6. When entering a new market, don't send out press releases too early

7. Sharks will not attack you if there is an easier target around

8. Don't act like a victim

9. Attack is good defence

10. Develop better escape tactics than the hunter

Introduction: Defence

Mankind's fear of a potential shark attack is enormous — therefore it made sense to develop this defence part of Sharkonomics. Read this part of the book to avoid giving the competition the edge of striking.

Both in nature and business prey and predator share the same water. Eventually all market leaders will be attacked as a consequence of being in the same market and sharing the same water as their predators. The concept behind developing brands was to protect the original from being copied. For a long time a brand relied on its name and reputation to survive in the market. Today, however, merely the name will not protect the brand from being attacked. As the nature of business gets harder, the need for defence increases. Market leaders need to defend their products and services with deadly seriousness to keep followers at a healthy distance.

Fear can hinder both organizations and individuals from developing further. Facing up to fear is a much better option than being in *denial of risk* as Jim Collins pointed out in his book *How the Mighty Fall.* Denial of risk is what shark experts would call *looking for trouble* – sharks know what's in the water and

they will use their skills to balance the odds. Mr Collins calls it: "taking risks below the waterline". All market leaders which want to remain at the top need to face their inevitable mortality.

Mankind's knowledge of the shark's defence is still at the trail-and-error stage. Those who fell into the error part are no longer around to share their knowledge – it's no wonder some survivors reported with all seriousness having seen the shark smiling at them.

Market leaders who have been attacked do not believe it will happen again to them, referring often to the saying: "lightning never strikes twice". Several divers have used the same denial strategy and jumped back into the water. In one such case nothing more than a leg was found after the second shark attack.[11] Bad defence is not good for market leaders; but it puts a smile on their competition.

> `Learning is never too late, but learning too slow is always too late.`

During World War II, the US Army published the classic shark survival manual[12] reasoning that if their soldiers ended up in deadly waters filled with sharks, they would know how to handle the sharks with some strategic survival moves:

> *Punch them on their vulnerable snout! Hold on to the shark's fin – it will swim down to rescue itself; let go when you think it has had enough!*

The survival manual worked in the sense that it made the soldiers face their worst fears. But when it came to a face-to-face boxing-match with a Great White Shark, the manual did not quite deliver what it was supposed to. The US Army's purpose at that time might have been to get soldiers to underestimate the risk and deny the size of the risk. But just as it was for the soldiers, this kind of denial will eventually lead to the fall of the market leaders.

Many others have tried to find the perfect shark defence – for example, dressing up in certain colours to disguise themselves as non-food to sharks. Some people have even suggested that human beings can outswim sharks (fear can make us believe anything). Moreover, some people believed that screaming underwater would scare the shark away. What I found as the most bizarre defence ever was playing Beatles music under the water.[13] The only proven effect these creative defence strategies had was to reduce mankind's feeling of being vulnerable under water. But sadly, many of these defences actually had the opposite effect and triggered several horrifying attacks.

I do not recommend any of the above shark defence strategies. Instead I have developed ten defence points against predator attacks. My goal with these defence points is to help market leaders to defend their territories and use the fear of an attack to inspire management to change in order to grow their businesses.

> *Strong defence will balance the arms race between predator and prey and will inspire market leaders to make some major evolutionary changes in the nature of business.*

Develop your defence strategies
years before you get attacked

Thinking outside the box is much
easier when swimming in the sea than
in an aquarium. Super predators
that have survived over hundreds of
millions of years did so because
their defence strategy was as strong
as their attack strategy.

It may sound ridiculous, but most of today's market leaders do not have any form of defence! Since market leaders hire me to question their business and attack them I can tell by experience that their defences do not exist (and if it does exist, it is not as strong as they believe). Why does an online search for *market leaders* only result in finding business websites, and a search for *market defence* only result in finding military defence websites? Simply because in business, defence is not highly valued and therefore not rewarded. In the military world, people will die if they don't have a good defence.

Name one winning sports team that does not have a good defence? Name one part of your organization or within your business field that deals with defence? Tell me the best "defence players" at today's *Fortune* 500 companies? There are no fancy business magazines writing about good defence players. Bad defence cost a fortune for market leaders such as BP, Toyota, HP, Apple, Microsoft, HD,

GM and IBM. After an attack it's often too late to establish your defence. It simply costs too much to rescue the victim. Or too much damage has been inflicted on some companies that they will never again become market leaders. Instead they become empty shells floating around in the water.

Why is defence not valued?

As early as in our childhood, from kindergarten upwards, we are trained to be "positive". So if somebody in the team building the mighty *Titanic* had said something that was not in line with "the unsinkable creation", that person would most likely have been put down and corrected (or at least sent off to clean the deck until he had learnt how to be more positive). Internal communications spend fortunes on rewriting information into a positive tone of voice. Initiatives such as bonus systems and stock values are popular in business because positive information can easily be aligned with payroll.

> In nature there are not any
> parachute agreements for management.

Researchers point out that many corporations have a climate of denial. Instead of confronting external threats and making the required decisions to adapt, they simply reorganize and restructure their internal reality.[14] If Nokia, Samsung and Motorola had a team playing defence, they would not have lost their market leader positions to Apple's iPhone. Developing defence skills is a natural part of the shark's nature and it should be a natural part of any corporation. By changing how we value defence we can plan and educate ourselves long before the attack is carried out.

There are disciplines in the martial arts that have so well-developed defence systems that the only way of carrying out a

good attack and still be able to walk home on both legs the same day is not to attack. Steve Jobs & co would not have attacked the mobile industry at that time if they knew it would cost them more than they would gain from the attack. Defence is perhaps even more important than attack when it comes to controlling a good feeding ground.

Too late is too dead

Far below Wall Street lurk dangerous shadows waiting for market leaders to make the wrong move. To deny you are potential prey only puts you on the menu. Instead, you should study competitors from within a shark cage so that you can get to know your predators. But don't feed them – shark experts warn that it is a bad idea to get sharks to associate you with shark food.

For predators it is important to study their prey so that they can learn how their prey moves, turns and adapts to different environmental changes. Both predator and prey are struggling to survive. The more danger the prey is facing the more skills are required to survive. In the world's most dangerous waters Great Whites are ambushing seals on the surface from deep below at high speed. In a split second before the deadly jaws dig deep into its flesh, the seal senses the shock wave as the shark cruises through the water to attack. In that split second there is no time for analyzing market research – moving too late is too dead!

Google's mortality v evolution

It was not long ago that many market leaders were described as superior in competition and immortal in various management books. Yet, many of these same companies have disappeared now. *Why?* Well, all living things eventually die. It's like the human body; it renews itself by regenerating its DNA.[15] It is this process that enables us to stay alive. But as we get older the renewing process in our body slows down, thus making the human body grow older. Aging leads to limited abilities in the human body; it's the same for companies when their corporate DNA is not renewed. Without change and innovation, a company will not regenerate its corporate DNA and, as a result, it starts to slow down.

Google regenerated itself by allowing employees to use 20% of their working time (one day per week) to work on new projects and ideas. That 20% also motivates Google's employees to work more effectively during the rest of the week.[16] They call it "new projects", but I would argue that moving is not an option for market leaders which want to stay alive. By working on its process of renewal, Google will grow its strength and defence capability.

Google maybe highly ranked by today's business media, but as an organization it is constantly dying 24/7. *Why?* Its top management and talent will not be around in 5–50 years' time depending on the circumstances and events Google finds itself in. If Google does not continue to attract new talent, its speed of development will slow down and eventually it will stop renewing itself. For predators it will be feeding time when Google's evolutionary speed begins to slow down. In evolution it is never a question of *if* they will slow down but it is always a question of *when* they will slow down.

02 Never stand still

Sharks love feeding on the carcasses of whales. When whales realize that their time is coming they simply swim up on to the beach — a better option than being eaten alive. Strategies for defence will help keep market leaders away from the crowded beaches where others are looking for a calm end.

Whales are fantastic creatures and play an important role in the ocean's ecosystem. But they are also the shark's largest prey. In business, the big whales are the big market leaders which are extremely nutritious and filled with fleshy market share.

        The time has come for market leaders
        to enter the beach.

The above is not true for all but true for those market leaders which stand still. In fact many market leaders are making themselves vulnerable to attack by not moving or by being too predictable in the moves they make. The old saying, "the bigger they are, the harder they fall", continues to be true and market leaders which don't wish to fall have to improve their market defence skills.

Why Microsoft was forced to improve its defence skills

Not so long ago Microsoft was a shark, superior to all competition. When Netscape's web browser was expanding fast, Microsoft moved in with Explorer and made a brutal killing. As Stephen Shankland of Cnet.com said: "Netscape was a key to making the World Wide Web useful…The software also struck fear into the heart of Microsoft, raising the prospect of a computing environment that could rival Windows. But Microsoft fought back with Internet Explorer, winning away Netscape's dominant market share."

At the beginning of Microsoft's successful hunting era, the company recruited super talented personnel, which made it easy for Microsoft to become an apex predator on the market. Eventually the tide changed and today Microsoft is swimming upstream against heavy resistance with its solutions and brand. *Why?* We live in a transparent market in a culture best described as open source, which is not an advantage for Microsoft. Being big often means having a hard time adjusting to change, especially change that occurs faster than the company's ability to adapt to it. But sometimes the mighty ones develop cultures that are unwilling to adapt (denial has that effect).

In today's deadly waters not even market leaders like Microsoft have a choice except to improve its defence skills unless it wants to be eaten alive like a whale carcass when the competition come calling. At the beginning of the open source revolution, Microsoft tried to defend its market share with pure denial and arrogance, which back-fired big time. When times change, it does not matter how mighty the market leader is. These companies need to change the direction of their solutions and follow the currents to where the market is taking them. If they don't they

will end up stranded on the beach. This is the simple reason for why Microsoft moved into open source and the reason for why it acquired Skype. The latter has the flavour of consumer power which Microsoft so desperately needed to add to its corporate DNA and survive in the seas it operated in. As Microsoft's CEO Steve Ballmer admitted: "Skype is a phenomenal service that is loved by millions of people around the world. "

The question Microsoft needs to answer is who loves Microsoft? If it can answer that question without having to pay for that love, Microsoft will engage followers to become a part of its defence. Those things you can't purchase (such as internal and external loyalty) tend to represent good defence. So long as its competitors do not organize themselves against Microsoft, or grow big enough to attack, Microsoft is quite safe. But it's only a matter of time when that will happen, so Microsoft has to keep developing its defence skills.

In nature life is always on the edge

Adaptability is not an option in nature. Either you are doing a good job or you are good meat for other sharks to feed on. Living in that kind of environment could be a bit stressful but still sharks always look deadly calm even in such environments. Being stressed may send a signal that you are vulnerable to attack. Even for sharks image is everything.

Why Sir Shark is always looking for market leaders who stand still

Throughout the world's ocean-markets Sir Richard Branson is looking for vulnerable market leaders to attack. In the beginning the mighty "whales" did not believe Sir Shark was capable of attacking them or moving in for the kill. They learned the hard way – today they have come to realize it is time to swim fast whenever Mr Branson's Virgin corporate red dorsal fin shows up. Some market leaders fear Mr Branson's unconventional attacks so much that they leave their territories and simply swim up on to the beach. *Why?* Because Sir Shark's strike record is a bloody story which by itself helps Virgin to win territories. This brutal reputation offers a strong dimension of defence, because others will not strike for fear of Virgin's counter attack.

> Those who move too slowly will put themselves on the menu of predators.

Nature's navigation system is based on movement

When you take a walk in the forest you will hear the birds singing and the wind blowing. For each step you take, the sound changes its direction. This is nature's way of creating a Global Positioning System (GPS) for the animal kingdom. The more you move, the more the environment updates your GPS about changes surrounding your movements. Suddenly silence will send a warning signal of a potential threat.

Imagine having the superior senses of a shark. As you are cruising through the sea and sensing the currents, water and electromagnetic fields, your senses are able to sense in a split second the different warning signals of an approaching threat. By comparing data from touch point positions in your internal GPS system you will have a 3-D picture of that potential threat. This will help you to understand better what is hunting you and how you should move out of its striking distance.

Market leaders often navigate with too few touch points. If they had more sources to create a 3-D picture, they would be able to find a way to escape or defend themselves.

2

Controlling your heartbeat v big trouble

As an attack approaches, it is crucial to manage the company's heartbeat in order to implement a good defence and not trigger the predator's instincts to attack. In an interview with Swedbank's CEO Michael Wolf, he mentioned how blogging internally to employees was crucial for opening up a dialogue with them. It was an excellent way of strengthening the company's culture, keeping people calm and increasing their performance and loyalty. Social media is a powerful tool to use for sending internal messages and has an important role to play in strengthening defences against external attack.

Let others spread the buzz

The movie *Jaws* induced such widespread fear that people opted to swim in swimming pools. In the movie there was one element that spread fear the most: that dull, heart-beating sound. People today still use it to symbolize fear or an approaching threat.

Back in 1975, when *Jaws* was making millions of people around the world scream out of fear, 3-D (three-dimensional) movies or superior sound systems like the THX did not exist in cinemas. What they had was an audience who like all creatures had a natural instinct for survival. Our survival instincts send out signals of fear to our senses faster than any 3-D system. By connecting the approaching shark with a unique sound, the producers did not even have to show the shark before fear and panic reached the audience. They pushed the audience's "fear button" without actually having to do anything other than creating a setting where our natural survival instincts were confronted with the threat of a potential predator eating us alive.

Like an early version of mind control, *Jaws* used manipulative methods to persuade us to sense real fear. *Jaws* was directed by Steven Spielberg who, without the aid of 3-D or THX, used plastic shark models (named Bruce, after the movie director's lawyer[17]) to play on people's fear.

Mr Spielberg was later known to have said that the film would only have been half as successful if it did not have the music composed by John Towner Williams. As a market defender, imagine what fear you can spread today. Back in 1975, they did not have the Internet, YouTube or any other social media tools to create and spread buzz. Fear is a natural survival instinct that can help you keep predators at a healthy distance.

> *Let potential predators sense their own fear every time they get near you.*

Predator's fear of counter-strikes is based on what they think their prey is capable of

Jaws terrified people all over the world. We fear the shark in the movie even though we hardly ever get to see it. Fear makes us believe in things that only exist in our minds. Scary movies base their horrifying stories on people's built-in fear button. The fear is never as strong as it is in our minds. But because all predators have strong survival instincts, fear can be a strong weapon of defence.

Make them pay the ultimate price for every attack

A hungry predator looking for a meal will look at potential prey and make its choice in the same way as we would read a restaurant menu. We would compare each item with the price we have to pay. If you make the predator believe that your price is too high, it will look at something else on the menu or maybe even go elsewhere.

Elephant Seals can weigh over three tons and are armed with strength and teeth to protect themselves. Not only do they protect themselves successfully but they are sometimes known to eat sharks. In many cases Elephant Seals will mark the shark with visible injuries during their counter-attack. This transforms the attacking shark into a visible billboard of how powerful your defence has proven to be. Leaving your attacker alive makes it easy for them to spread the buzz about your defence capabilities. Overall, it will discourage other attackers from seeing you as an easy and cheap meal.

Sharks aren't maniac killers; they don't kill for no apparent reason; they kill to eat. The more energy it takes or the more risky it is to attack a certain prey, the more likely they will seek other prey than your business. This is part of the reason why sharks prefer young seals, which have less experience and don't yet understand the risks they are taking and therefore are more willing to take bigger risks. Dress and behave in an experienced manner and these predators will not target you as their first choice.

Teamworking is a strong form of defence

An effective way of showing a shark that attacking would mean trouble is teamworking. Sharks know that a pack (team) increases the risk of it suffering from counter attacks from others in that team. The power of whistleblowers effectively works like a sonar system online. Whistleblower organizations such as WikiLeaks. org have proven that the power of information can impact and inspire change. There are over 100 million blogs in the world and each one of them can function as a whistleblower warning you when a predator is getting too close.

Market leaders which don't feel they have strong market defences can do what small fish do in the sea – swim together so that they look bigger and stronger than they actually are. An effective way of doing this is to be in a network. Motorcycles gangs have on their jackets symbols that imply to others: if you attack me, the others will eat you up like raw sushi.

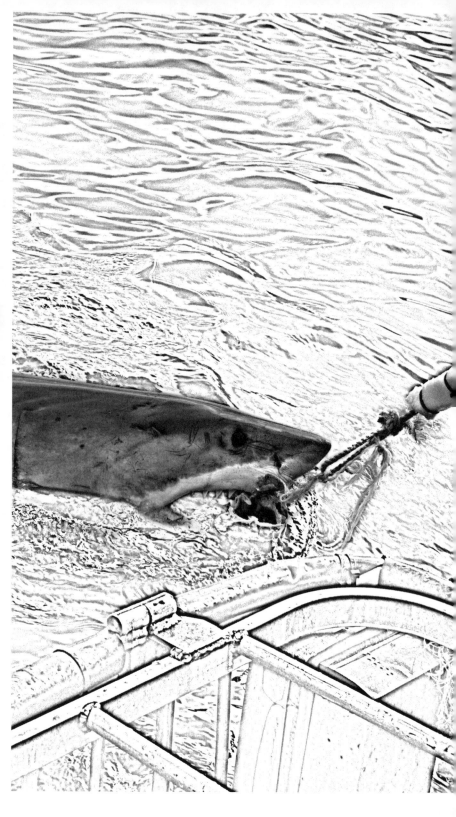

Don't panic when under shark attack

04

After taking a test-bite the attack is not over. The attacker is only waiting for you to lower the price they have to pay before making the final kill (often referred to as the shark's bait-and-wait strategy). Be prepared but don't panic — control your core business and move out of reach.

A bite is a bite and it does not have much to do with the size of the shark. A test-bite in itself does not need to be bad news – but the effect of blood in the water is always bad news.

> "For an information crime to reach the surface, something drastic must happen. When it does, the results tend to be pretty revealing"
> — Steven Levitt and Stephen Dubner, Freakonomics.

Move out of reach

If you are in shark water you have to accept the fact that you're on the menu. Being on the market has a price; the more money there is in your territory, the more sharks it will attract. Every shark bite is an indication that you have something worth defending.

Market leaders could test their defences by encouraging small competitors to enter into their market territories (for example, by lowering distribution barriers). It will speed up their process of learning about defence. Organizations which are kept on their toes will be better prepared and able to move out of the reach of predators.

Using bait to defend territory

Australian shark hunter Vic Hislop used an effective but controversial technique to hunt sharks which resulted in a world record for catching Great White Sharks. Mr Hislop used a live shark attached to a floating oil drum. While connected to the drum, the bait shark was able to attack anything smaller than itself; but when it came to bigger sharks, it was helpless. A cruel but effective way of catching big sharks.

This is an effective defence strategy which can be transformed into a business strategy. Put out "bait sharks" around your core business and attach them to a floating oil drum. The only attacker that can make the oil drum move is a shark big enough to be a real threat to your territory dominance. In the meantime, you can keep focusing on your feeding ground. In dangerous waters you need to build aggressive defence lines around your territory business. The business bait can be smaller B2B or B2C relationships which are loyal, especially if their very survival depends on keeping you alive.

Mr Hislop expressed his admiration for one of the sharks in his collection: "I'm planning to freeze it and then put it on display at the shark museum."[18] A good idea for market leaders who want to display their defence capabilities at the front entrance of their headquarters. At the time when Mr Hislop started his hunting career, sharks were not highly valued creatures – today

we value and respect nature's resources more than putting them in a museum.

Killing sharks today is so controversial that Mr Hislop got his own anti-groups on Facebook. The comments are not quotable here except for one nice one by Martin Bannard: "We evolved out of the ocean, and the shark stayed in it."[19]

Making territory less attractive

"Sharks are going to feed, as long as there is food in the water" (from the movie *Jaws*). By decreasing the amount of food in your territory, you automatically make it less attractive to hunt in. Sharks don't stick around to starve.

By lowering the prices in your territory fewer predators will find profitability in your business field. This defence skill is performed very well by the likes of Wal-Mart, Carrefour, Tesco, IKEA, H&M, Topshop, Media Markt, all of whom have lowered their prices so low that it has effectively killed off the competition. Local market leaders are often not capable of competing with global players (but even the mightiest ones started locally). Global players can afford to get bitten a thousand times, bleed endlessly and still survive.

For local market leaders there are always ways to protect their market against global players. McDonald's learned this the hard way when consumers preferred the local Swedish MAX hamburgers over McDonald's. In one part of Sweden the biggest player of them all could not win over the local hero's struggles to survive. This struggling small brand (MAX) has now grown into a national competitor that may swim globally in the future. McDonald's is learning its lessons too slow and as a result it has cost it market share.

Find out where your blind spots are

05

There are at least 500 blind spots amongst the Fortune 500. From their headquarters market leaders don't see their blind spots. The more distant they are to their market, the more vulnerable they become. Don't go looking for trouble. Test and educate your business to adapt before it's too late.

Mighty market leaders always face the risk of bureaucratic processes and internal politics slowing down the speed of their corporate evolution. When that happens, they will have the smell of prey about them. Instead of allowing a culture of denial to set in, corporations can use attacks (and potential ones) to help them turn their weaknesses into a stronger market defence. No matter what kind of attack it faces, the corporation can learn from it and seek out the positives in order to strengthen its defence.

Move out of G-attack into G-defence to counter attack in a "killer loop"

When predators are circling their prey, their goal is to locate the prey's blind spot. For the prey, instead of standing still in the market, it is better to try to break up the attacker's pattern before it is too late. It does not matter if the size of the attacker is enormous. Every attacker has a vulnerable part that can be bitten off (for example, attacking its core business).

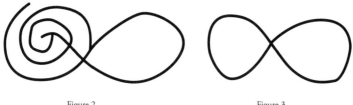

Figure 2   Figure 3

Figures 2-3: When the attacker moves in a G-attack, you should move out (Figure 2) and go into a "killer loop" (Figure 3).

Normally the attacker will start swimming around its prey with a view to remaining undetected. By disrupting the predator's swimming pattern and moving out of striking distance (Figure 2), safety can be achieved. Then by turning around (in a "killer loop"), a counter attack is possible for the prey against the attacker (Figure 3). G2G (G-attack into G-defence) is best performed when your attacker believes it is in stealth mode (and believes its prey cannot see it), when in fact you *can* see your attacker coming.

Rent out your blind spots to defenders

When IKEA builds a new retail store, it doesn't rent a shop. Instead it buys its own land and uses a part of that land to build its shop on. The rest of its land is rented out to other retailers which are willing to pay rent to be in IKEA's feeding grounds. These retailers are not competitors of IKEA. Since IKEA is attracting huge numbers of consumers, the other retailers in its domain are loyal enough to defend IKEA. Loyalty is often strongest when it is well rewarded with nutritious consumers to feed on. Who said good defence can't be profitable?

Outsourcing weakness

Surrounding each market leader is an ecosystem of suppliers working in a B2B (business-to-business) relationship. Some have developed a strong defence around its market share without actually having to expend its own resources. Sharks outsource their weaknesses to other fish in order to keep them clean and protected from disease. These fish help the sharks stay healthy hunters. Apple has the same strategy. Around its products are other brands supplying parts of the solution: Kensington makes the keyboard for the iPad; Harman Kardon makes the speakers; Belkin makes products for the iPhone, iPad and iPod; and Logitech makes the most out of every opportunity Apple offers it.

IKEA also outsources its weaknesses to other "fish": Parts of Sweden makes unique furniture solutions and products to complement IKEA's range of solutions; Bemz makes the slipcover for IKEA sofas, which results in more variation and consumer choice in design.

Not all consumers want or have the time to transport and assemble their IKEA furniture, so IKEA has outsourced this service to local suppliers (or else consumers may choose to buy furniture which is already assembled from a competitor of IKEA's).

The above suppliers are not a threat, rather they give strength and support to the market leaders. They also function as an inspirational R&D department. As long as these suppliers are running their businesses in a way that benefits market leaders, they function as a means for market leaders to outsource their weaknesses and therefore strengthen their defences. Just as sharks let other fish protect them and clean away their problems, these suppliers compensate for the market leaders' weaknesses and cover up their blind spots.

Sharks for rent

Just as market leaders hire me to detect their blind spots, they can hire sharks to protect and guard their weaknesses. If McDonald's had teamed up with a local shark to compete with MAX hamburgers in Sweden, McDonald's could have succeeded in slowing down the development of their attackers. Since the big players have problems adapting quickly, "sharks for rent" can make sense sometimes. By rewarding other sharks to protect your territory, you will have enough time to develop defence skills to protect your blind spot weakness. If these sharks fail and get killed whilst defending your territory, their stomachs will at least reveal the kind of threat you are facing which can be a good alternative to traditional market research data. If McDonald's had rented sharks, it could have prevented all that time wasted on developing an offer which consumers only eventually came to accept.

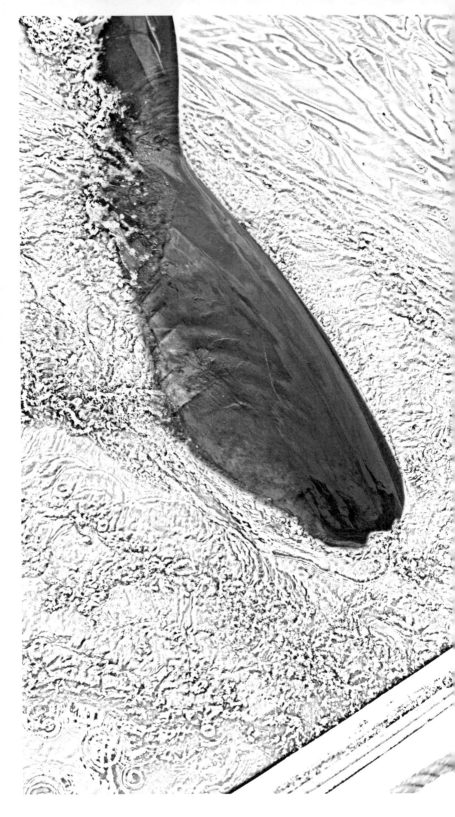

When entering a new market, don't send out press releases too early

Business competitors act like sharks. They can also sense as little as one drop of blood in the water and a press release is more than a drop of blood. It will not take competitors long before they enter the new market. When Apple reported the success of its iPad, it was like pouring blood into an ocean, attracting hungry competitors into Apple's new territory and turning a profitable feeding ground into deadly shark waters.

Territories that smell are looking for trouble

Territories with few market leaders often contain very little competition. Sharks can't resist the scent of market share and potential profits floating around in the water like dead meat.

Market leaders often feel immortal and do not see the threats lurking beneath the surface. If they would bother to look below the surface, they would see a shadow gliding elegantly around them in stalking mode, learning and developing its skills. The music industry should have seen Apple circling around it years before the latter's attack.

When music stars such as Bon Jovi describe how Apple killed the music industry, they are really only referring to the fact that iTunes & co have now entered into their feeding ground. When the game changes, it forces you to innovate. Hence, Bon Jovi developed a broader line of merchandising products via Bonjovi. com beyond its music. Mr Jovi has increased his control over the market by having a direct online dialog with his fans. Online offers such as membership packages and access to backstage have got fans to sign up and transform their admiration for Mr Jovi into cash.

Send out press releases when you're ready to eat

Only when your defence is strong is it time to send out press releases (the business equivalent of chumming for – or luring – sharks). Pouring blood into the water is a good idea if you have established good defence in your territories (having the resources to be mean). Since you never know what kind of predators the blood you poured will attract, it is important to have strong relationships with sharks in the market which can help you to protect your territories. But make sure you let your allies know you are inviting competitors into your territory.

If Apple had done its homework properly before pouring blood in the water, it would have secured its sales, production and distribution of iPad globally so that neither Motorola, HTC, LG nor Samsung would have had the chance to take any part of the market.

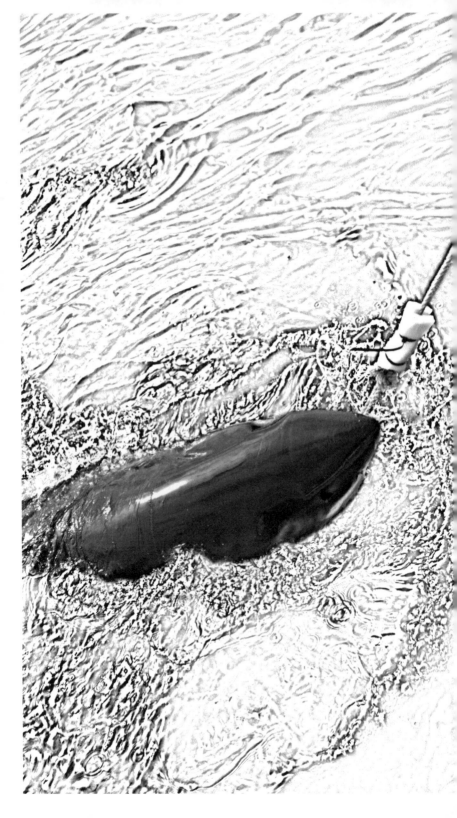

Sharks will not attack you if there is an easier target around

Sharks prefer fleshy nutritious prey. When your diving friend asks you to join him for a swim, make sure that your friend has more flesh to offer.

In the movie *Jaws 2* the diving instructor was shouting to the divers: "Let's buddy up and drop". What they did not know at that time was that Jaws was lurking beneath the boat. Those divers who buddied up with more fleshy ones had better defence odds than others. Bad or good luck is dependant on your choice of buddy. The same goes for business.

Why Steve Jobs had more luck

Few decision makers are as good as Steve Jobs was when it comes to doing the right thing at the right time. Mr Jobs connected the dots in a way that others don't. There was something magical about Steve Jobs in his ability to know what works and what doesn't. That gut feeling is not based on pure luck; part of it comes by training his senses when analyzing nearly everything around and in the waters of Apple Inc. Mr Jobs not only connected the dots in the present but also in relation to history and the future.

"You can't connect the dots looking
forward; you can only connect them
looking backwards"
— *Steve Jobs, speech at Stanford University,
14 June 2005.*

Today, many decision-makers base their decisions on too few facts and don't take enough notice of what is going on around them. Steve Jobs, however, was a perfectionist whose decision-making was based on almost every fact that he could get into his magical sonar system. Business leaders need to develop that sonar system as part of their defence.

Internal predatory combat

Try shouting "Shark!" in a swimming pool and probably no one will believe you because denying the risk is more comfortable. Place a shark in the same pool and return a week later, then it will be enough to whisper "Shark" to get people to walk on water. In every major organization there is internal fighting over budgets, power and sometimes egos. These fights are as deadly as the external shark attacks. Winning internal predatory fights is basically achieved in the same way as winning external ones. The difference lies in the elements; internal ones are based on corporate culture, climate and politics. Bureaucratic obstacles are great internal killers. Use those variables to make others the target of attacks rather than yourself.

When the hunter gets hunted in social media

Bad visibility is an advantage for sharks because they have superior senses. Social media works like a sonar system, where the hunter is looking for its prey. By sending out friendly signals you can make sharks focus their sonar system on your competitors. Social media can in this way work as a restaurant menu for cannibalism and, so long as they don't find you on that social media menu, you're safe. Mapping out the next moves of your competitors will make them an easy meal for other predators. Social media platforms such as Facebook and Linkedin are perfect defence tools you can use to put others on the menu.

Write about your nutritious friend on Facebook

Since sharks prefer fleshy prey, write about your nutritious competitors on the friend wall. Make sure to tag photos of your nutritious friends on Facebook. But don't do it in a way that others will see you as an anti-friend. Instead, make it look like a friendly bump (poke) – for example, your friend is "trying to lose weight". Sharks are good at helping out in that field.

08 Don't act like a victim

Market leaders often claim their defence is state-of-the-art until they are bleeding in the water. Bad defence can trigger sharks to attack. Acting like a victim will put even the mightiest on the menu of a predator.

Don't go swimming in market territories where there is a lot of shark food without sharpening your teeth and defence skills. Lots of shark-attack victims didn't know or were wrongly informed about what could trigger an attack. One important rule: Never buy advice from consultants who call themselves former shark experts or those who have had their scuba-diving equipment turned into pieces by sharks as they might be recognized as shark food.

A good team always has a strong defence

The business world is full of prominent attackers whose role in the organization is essentially to roll out market leaders all over the world. Basically people who are only working in one dimension are also good at creating blind spots in their own defences, which makes them vulnerable to attack. In sport there are no great teams that do not have a strong defence. Market leaders have a lot to learn from sport teams in order to balance their business results.

Check your scoreboard in defence

The NHL hockey team San Jose Sharks, through its website www.sanjosesharks.com, has built a strong team culture of defence, by giving its forwards and its defensive players the same level of importance. The team also invites its fans to play a role in its fanzone and community on the website, thus making the fans feel a part of the team. Being *one* internally and externally inspires everyone to be loyal to the team. The culture of defence is also powered by fan-websites such as www.fearthefin.com and www.arcticicehockey.com where fans analyze every part of their Shark's defence team in articles such as "Is the Sharks defence bad?"[20] Market leaders today also need to check their defence scoreboard to analyze if their team is a winner in defence or not.

Low internal loyalty leads to market leader suicide

Sharks move 24/7; lowly motivated employees don't. Instead, lowly motivated employees eventually start acting like victims who look for trouble by punishing consumers and clients. This level of loyalty is not always as destructive as it may sound. Loyal, desperate employees can sometimes do this as a defensive reflex to prove that change is needed. It is their way of pouring blood into the water in order to provoke a test bite. This in an internal way of chumming for management to address problems before it's too late and the company comes under external attack. Who said creating trouble can't be an effective way for change management to happen?

> Motivation is pure power,
> competitive competition is
> empowering that power.

Deal with the mighty, to learn from the best

The mightiest market leaders today are doing some things right. Playing in the NHL means playing against the best. Without that professional combat level, the San Jose Shark's performance would not be at the level which is needed in order to compete in the NHL. Market leaders who like to compete at the highest levels in their sectors need to find large and mean predators to test and stress their defence.

How Intel Inside creates strong defence on the outside

Defending a territory takes strength and resources. A way to gain this effectively is by outsourcing your defence to market leaders. One way to motivate them to defend you is to have a common goal (give them a reason to protect you and they will do so).

In the computer market, Intel's Inside brand is making weaker brands stronger on the outside and able to compete with the best in their field. Even mighty Google is using the "inside defence strategy" to move in the deadly waters of the mobile market by providing Samsung, HTC and others with its Android software.

Today both Intel and Android have grown into powerful players on their own which can easily move from being "inside" to attacking on the outside.

Attack is good defence

Prey and predator share the same waters.
Therefore, it is only a matter of time
before the two bump into each other. When
that happens, it is better to be the
first-mover in order to gain advantage.

When making the first move, it is important to be superior in speed, skill, resources and technology, or in anything else that creates advantage for you. Moreover, timing is crucial, especially if it is combined with any form of market change or trend in the environment within or around your territory. Major market changes – such as economic recessions, mergers/fusions, ownership changes, legal and political changes – will encourage predators to take bigger risks and greater number of attacks. Market leaders should capitalize on change to enable them to defend their territories and grow their business.

Killing with superiority

In a transparent market, the original brand is the one that delivers the most. When the nature of business gets harder, market leaders need to defend their products/services with deadly seriousness and intent. Having the legal rights or patent to a brand is no longer enough to scare off potential predators.

Instead, it can be the trigger for them to move in for a good meal. Market leaders need to evolve fast through innovation. Speed is not only required to keep up with the competition, it also creates a distance edge between you and your predators. It will cost attackers more energy to catch up with you than what they will gain from taking a bite of your market share. Remember: predators dislike spending more than they gain from the hunt.

Act like a predator

Predators have a gentleman's agreement between them: they don't attack or kill each other. There is practical sense in such an arrangement. Predators are not looking for trouble, they are looking for food. As a market leader, you can take advantage of this gentleman's agreement by disguising yourself just like a predator. Mirror your predators by doing what they do: have your office in Upper Manhattan; be seen having lunch with the top corporate lawyers; dress in power suits. Masquerading around as a predator, seemingly capable of killing even the strongest amongst them, will put off most predators from troubling you.

Markets leaders should use online social media

Predators often study their prey from a safe distance in the beginning, so that they can judge if the market leader is a threat or an easy target. They will start by researching through social media and then move closer, before finally ending up on the market leader's website. Through social media, market leaders can equally fend off potential predators. Put up case studies on your website, which demonstrate (with a strong warning) how you repelled previous attacks on your market share, or information about the level of investment required to compete in the market, or indeed an indication of what it would cost predators in terms of failure.

Smiling is good defence

Finally, don't underestimate smiling as a form of defence. When attacking, the last thing any predator expects is to be greeted with a smile from its prey. During attack, it is essential you stay calm, in control and confident before your predator. Moreover, don't look scared. A smiling, confident and unafraid prey no longer seems an easy meal for the predator, which is then more likely to look elsewhere.

Develop better escape tactics than the hunter

10

Do whatever it takes to not be on the top of the predator's attack list. Move in stealth mode if you're on the *Fortune* 500 list. Always be the number two choice predators would want to hunt. Make the predators attack Apple, Google, Audi and the other 497 market leaders before they hunt you. If you're not on the *Fortune* 500 list you're on some other attack list.

Innovating is a good way to escape or to move beyond striking distance, before a stalking predator uncovers your blind spots and moves in for the kill. In other words, it is never a mistake to be a good swimmer.

Good defence relies on knowledge and constantly searching for weaknesses. The following lists will help raise your awareness of potential threats and attackers. It will focus your mind on preventing attacks and entering the denial stage.

How to find out more about your attackers

1. Go online.
2. Search the *Fortune* 500. Read about them like a motivation menu – study and learn defence from them.
3. Pick your potential attackers on the menu and learn defence from them.
4. Start to work on your defence by using the *Sharkonomics* defence list from step one (see below).
5. Always bear in mind, even if you have succeeded in defending yourself against a strong attacker, there are still a lot more out there to defend yourself against.

Sharkonomics defence list

1. Start planning long before you are attacked.
2. Sharks will not attack you if there is an easier target around.
3. G-defence – practice your escape moves.
4. Practice the "killer loop".
5. Find your blind spots and protect them – take away your weak spots and your armour of defence will grow strong.
6. Build alliances with strong defenders.
7. Timing is the key for successful defence.
8. Move or die.
9. Never forget to be curious and have fun when killing your attacker.

Who are your top ten potential attackers to defend against?

1.
2.
3.
4.
5.
6.
7.
8.
9.
10.

Then move on to defence against others attackers.

What are your biggest blind spots?
1.
2.
3.
4.
5.
6.
7.
8.
9.
10.

Always do more than these lists and never ever stand still.

Check for more ways to avoid attacks and updates at www. Sharkonomics.com.

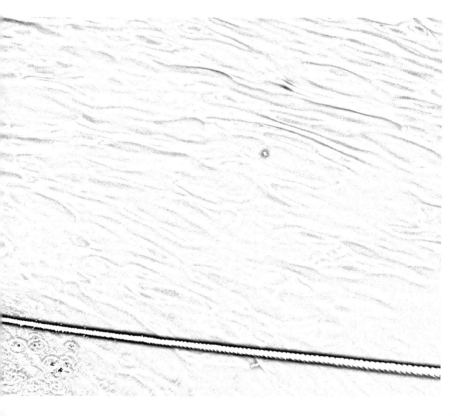

Mother Nature's endword

In 1968, Andy Warhol (1928–87) created the classic statement *"15 minutes of fame"*. Moreover, in 2007, in the movie *The Eleventh Hour*, scientists symbolically represented Earth's existence in 24 hours. Of these 24 hours, mankind's existence came to a total of only 15 minutes.

Since we are a young species on Earth, we have a lot to learn from sharks which have been around for more than 420 million years. If we (the "15 minutes species") exterminate the top predator of the sea, the Great White Shark, we may not survive as a species for more than 16 minutes.

Great White Shark experts such as Leonard Compagno, George Burgess, Michael Rutzen, Chris and Monique Fallows, Richard Ellis and Ron and Valerie Taylor are changing people's opinions about sharks. My ambition with *Sharkonomics* is to change our attitude towards learning from this animal. I have targeted readers from the business world, those who have the capital to change how things are done.

Whether I have succeeded or not is up to you, but for certain I have learned more from this exciting creature than I shall ever do from my fellow kind.

Acknowledgments

Extra thanks to my publisher and hero Martin Liu at Marshall Cavendish International. My super-mentor, Claes Andréasson. My family (including everything in the universe). My girlfriend for saving my dorsal fin and supporting me in life and book ambitions. My dyslexia. Shark experts Leonard Compagno, George Burgess, Chris and Monique Fallows, Michael Rutzen, Richard Ellis, Andre Hartman and Ron and Valerie Taylor. Peter Benchley.

Steven Spielberg, Roy Scheider, Lorraine Gary, Sam Quint, Emanuel Rosen, Kaj Arnö, Michael Wolf. Thom Thavenius. Paul Holman, Pekka Pohjakallio. Thanks to everyone I have interviewed for this book.

Professor Philip Kotler, Brian Solis, Eirik Hokstad, Martin Deinoff, Jesper Ek, Mariann Eriksson, Tom Asacker, Magnus Kroon, Calle Sjoenell, Kevin Lane Keller, Alan Gregerman, Charlotte Wik, Jan Fager, Carlos Viladevall Passola, Carl Wåreus, Colvyn Harris, Manoj Aravindakshan, Yann Mauchamp, Micael Dahlén, David Magliano, Alf Rehn, Ritva Hanski-Pitkäkoski, Stephen Brown, Nilgun Carlson, Jenny Näslund, Gisle Dueland,

From left to right: Stefan Engeseth with shark experts Chris Fallows, Michael Rutzen and Andre Hartman.

Evert Gummesson, Akram Raffoul, Derrick Daye, Jan Morten Drange, Martin Lindeskog, Johnnie Moore, Jack Yan, Ami Hasan, Luis-Daniel Alegria and Anna Söby.

Seth Godin, Jörgen Wahl, Per Nilsson, Jonas Nilsson, Sergej, Carin Balfe Arbman, Martin Lindeskog, Thomas Klamell, Roland Williams, Pär Lager, Sylvia Nylin, Anders Ericson, Bugge, Per Rosvall, Pia Grahn Brikell, Cannes Lions, Merci Olsson, Ulf Carlson, Dallas, Erik Dahlberg, Bengt Jönsson, Maria Forssén, Anna Caracolias, Walter, Huldt-Ramberg's. Gregerman's. Björkholtz's. Petrovski's, Söder's, OnTime, Strålfors, Binero, Reffekt.

A special thanks to Mother Nature for sharing your gift and nature of the Great White Shark.

All trademarks in this book are acknowledged as belonging to their respective companies.

Most of all, I would like to thank *you* for taking the time to read this book.

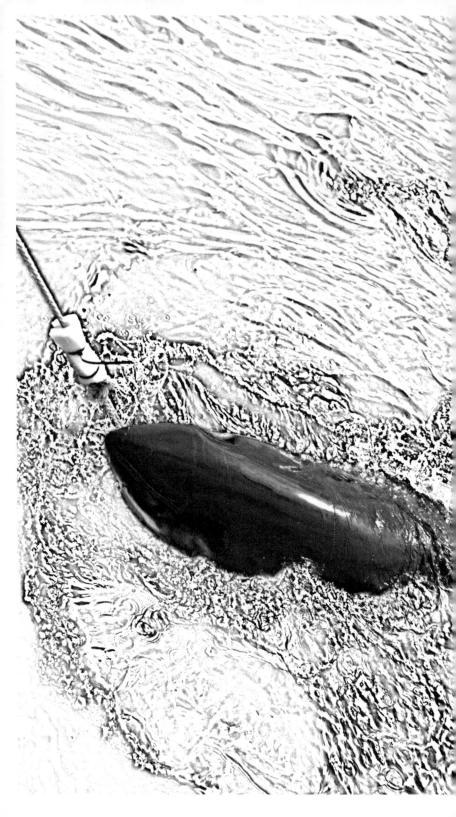

Recommended reading

Chris Anderson. *Free* (Hyperion, 2010).

Chris Anderson. *The Long Tail* (Hyperion, 2006).

Jim Collins. *How the Mighty Fall: And why some companies never give in* (Random House, 2009).

Richard Ellis & John McCosker. *Great White Shark* (Stanford University Press, 1995).

Malcolm Gladwell. *The Tipping Point* (Back Bay Books, 2002).

Peter Benchley. *Jaws* (Andre Deutsch, 1974).

Jaws. Movie directed by Steven Spielberg (1975).

Guy Kawasaki. *Enchantment* (Portfolio, 2011).

Guy Kawasaki. Lecture at Gulltaggen (April 27-29, 2010).

A. Pete Klimley. *The Secret Life of Sharks* (Simon & Schuster, 2007).

Steven D. Levitt & Stephen J. Dubner. *Freakonomics* (William Morrow, 2005).

Emanuel Rosen. *The Anatomy of Buzz* (Crown Business, 2009).

Emanuel Rosen. Interview (October 11, 2009).

Brian Solis. *Engage* (Wiley, 2010).

Brian Solis. Interview and lecture at World Public Relations Forum (June 13, 2010).

Wikipedia.org. *Key words connected to sharks* (2011).

Notes

1. Xavier Maniguet. *The Jaws of Death* (Skyhorse Publishing, 2007).
2. Michael Capuzzo. *Close to Shore: The terrifying shark attacks of 1916* (Broadway, 2002).
3. Robert Frenay. *Pulse: The coming age of systems and machines inspired by living things* (Bison Books, 2008).
4. Michael Rothschild. *Bionomics* (Futura Publications, 1992).
5. Wikipedia.org. Key word: Sharks. http://en.wikipedia.org/wiki/Sharks (2011).
6. Budweiser.com.http://www.budweiser.com/en/our-legacy/adolphus-busch-our-founding-father/default.aspx#/our-legacy/american-ingenuity/index (2011).
7. Hugh Edwards. *Shark: The shadow below* (HarperCollins, 1998).
8. Seth Godin. *Tribes: We need you to lead us* (Portfolio, 2008).
9. Torill Kornfeldt. Article: Most Predators Are Cannibal (Research & Advances/Forskning & Framsteg (Issue nr 2, 2011).
10. Mike Butcher. Article: Oracle To Buy Sun For Approximately $7.4 Billion (Techcrunch.com, 2009).

11. Ellis & McCosker. *Great White Shark* (Stanford University Press, 1995).
12. Xavier Maniguet. *The Jaws of Death* (Skyhorse Publishing, 2007).
13. Xavier Maniguet. *Ibid.*
14. Jim Collins. *How the Mighty Fall: And why some companies never give in* (Random House, 2009).
15. Bruce M. Carlson. *Principles of Regenerative Biology* (Academic Press, 2007).
16. Daniel H. Pink. *Drive* (Riverhead Trade, 2011).
17. Neil Smith. Article: Shark Tale that Changed Hollywood (Bbc.co.uk, June 3-2005).
18. Richard Shears. Article: You'll Never Guess What I Caught Today: The giant hammerhead shark hauled from the deep (Dailymail.co.uk, April 16, 2010).
19. Martin Bannard. (Facebook.com, April 29, 2011).
20. Hawerchuk. Article: Is the Sharks Defense Bad? (Arcticicehockey.com, January 5, 2011).

About the author

Author, consultant and speaker Stefan Engeseth works and lectures internationally, and is based in Stockholm, Sweden. Over the years, Stefan has worked as a consultant for international and *Fortune* 500 corporations.

He is often described as one of the world's leading experts and speakers in his field. His ideas range from innovative and future-oriented to bordering on the far-fetched. Yet, they all build on the universal truth that without innovation and vision, companies will not grow in today's highly competitive business world. The question is how far you are prepared to go. Stefan Engeseth is the founder and CEO of Detective Marketing™, a consulting firm that helps companies around the world find new business opportunities in areas such as strategy, business development, branding, communications and marketing. Market leaders often

hire Stefan to attack their businesses, spot their weaknesses and prepare them for competitive attack. He is also a creative advisor to a number of environmental and charitable organizations.

Stefan Engeseth is the author of three other acclaimed books: *Detective Marketing, ONE* and *The Fall of PR and the Rise of Advertising.*

Stefan Engeseth is one of Europe's most creative business thinkers and a top-ranked speaker.

He can be reached at www.DetectiveMarketing.com.

Or take a bite at www.Sharkonomics.com.